# SEASONS
## an inspirational journey

# SEASONS
## an inspirational journey

Mette Ahlefeldt-Laurvig

Photography
Hans Ole Madsen

Lime Walk Press

SEASONS – an inspirational journey

© Mette Ahlefeldt-Laurvig, 2009

Text and idea: Mette Ahlefeldt-Laurvig
Photography: Hans Ole Madsen
Design & styling: Mette Ahlefeldt-Laurvig &
Hilary Watson
English editor: Katie Schwarck
Layout: Annette Bjerre Design
English layout consultant: Sally Hughes

Danish Edition: ISBN 87-11-18143-5
German Edition: ISBN-13: 9783512032868

A catalogue record for this book is available
from the British Library

Mette Ahlefeldt-Laurvig asserts the moral right to be
identified as the author of this work

Printed and bound in Denmark by Narayana Press

ISBN 978-0-9563438-0-2


Lime Walk Press
www.limewalkpress.com

For William, Stoffer and Stanci
and for all our trips down the Thames

# CONTENTS

## Spring

## Summer

# Autumn

## 108

# Winter

## 156

SEASONS is a celebration of the English countryside.

Little prepared me for the impact of moving from London to lush, green Oxfordshire some nine years ago. Wherever I turned there was beauty: fine manor houses with rose walks and ha-has and charming cottages with delightful country gardens. There was timelessness and history and loveliness all around. I was instantly smitten. Nine years down the line have done little to dampen my enthusiasm. While I used to think British villages the most attractive in the world I now *know* they are. I hope my foreign roots – a Dane with twenty years of living in England – will go some way to explaining this fulsome praise. But it can't be helped; the British countryside is indeed unsurpassed and this book is my personal tribute.

SEASONS is arranged as a creative logbook, drawing inspiration from nature and my immediate surroundings. Each season is introduced by a mood board that encapsulates the essence of the particular time of year as I see it. Living in the countryside means there is never a shortage of inspiration. Flowers are an obvious source, but, beautiful as they are, I also like to look for patterns in the way, for instance, garden tools hang on a wall, in the structure of the underside of a mushroom, in drops of rain or on a horse's coat. The following pages offer many examples of how to adapt such motifs and use them in interior design and decoration.

Another aspect of this book is the garden itself. In tune with the four seasons, I have included practical gardening tips and as I am the fortunate owner of a kitchen garden, it is perhaps inevitable that some of my favourite recipes have also found their way into these pages.

As a lover of history, an additional joy of writing this book was to discover more about England's heritage, so deeply embedded in its fine country houses and gardens. I have attempted to convey some of the more unusual customs and traditions in pictures and anecdotes and there may even be snippets of new information for the British reader.

SEASONS has truly been an inspirational journey. I hope the reader will indulge me in my celebration of the English countryside.

Mette Ahlefeldt-Laurvig

# The spirit of spring

A meadow golden with buttercups. The dazzling colour and heady scent confirm
that spring has finally arrived. The countryside beckons and offers new inspiration.
Now is the time to take out your sketchbook, fill your house with flowers and
introduce a palette of fresh spring colours into your home.

# Spring

Nothing is so beautiful as Spring

When weeds, in wheels, shoot long and lovely and lush;

Thrush's eggs look little low heavens, and thrush

Through the echoing timber does so rinse and wring

The ear, it strikes like lightnings to hear him sing;

The glassy peartree leaves and blooms, they brush

The descending blue; that blue is all in a rush

With richness; the racing lambs too have fair their fling.

Gerard Manley Hopkins
(1844–1889)

Spring in Oxfordshire

### A manor house

The Oxfordshire countryside offers one delightful village after another. Pretty cottages, charming gardens, beautiful churches and handsome manor houses.

In days gone by, the lord of the manor usually owned the entire village and the 'manor' referred to all his land not just the main house on his estate. Nowadays, a manor evokes a picture of an old rambling house, quietly tucked away, with that lived-in quality that only time can bestow.

### The English cottage

What could be more quintessentially English than a thatched cottage? Layers of thatch follow every curve as if moulded by hand. And it is practical too, as the flexible, lightweight straws are ideal for rickety old walls that would struggle to support a heavy roof.

### Little Wittenham Manor

In medieval times, the village of Little Wittenham, including the grange next to the church, was owned by Abingdon Abbey. In 1552, Mr William Dunch of London purchased the estate from the Crown and built Little Wittenham Manor. The Wittenham estate fell into the hands of Henry VIII during his dissolution of the monasteries and is one of many examples of 'Old Coppernose' making a handsome profit from severing England's ties with the Catholic Church.

### Mrs Jarvis from Philadelphia

A century ago, a Mrs Jarvis believed that America should honour the unsung work of mothers. After her death, her daughter eventually managed to persuade Congress to establish a Mother's Day on the second Sunday in May, the date of Mrs Jarvis' death. A hundred years on, this day is now celebrated in large parts of the world, but Britain retains its own Mothering Sunday.

### A nosegay for mother

A posy of primrose, periwinkle, anemone and grape hyacinths.

### Mothering Sunday in England

One would be forgiven for assuming that Mothering Sunday and Mother's Day are identical. They're not. Falling on the fourth Sunday of Lent, Mothering Sunday marks the day when children were granted a day off work to visit their mother. They often brought with them a posy of hand-picked flowers. The forerunner of this custom is the much older tradition of visiting the 'mother church', the nearest large church, during Lent. Children would pick flowers to decorate the church or to give to their mother. As they still do today.

### The scent of spring

They are such wonderful har-bingers of spring, the hyacinths. Blooming as early as March they disappear all too soon. Although the South of England is just mild enough, they prefer warmer climes.

### Decorating Easter eggs

Decorating eggs is fun, particularly when the business of egg blowing is over and done with. These eggs have been given two coats of acrylic paint in soft pastel tones and are ready for decoration. For a three dimensional effect use fabric paints, which come in tubes and are easy to use. Some of them contain a mother of pearl effect, which will add sparkle to the surface, as will small glass beads. Pull a metal thread through the holes in the eggs to hang them. Secure the thread at the top and bottom using a golden bead. Add a metal 'crown' from a jewellery kit at the top to create an attractive finish.

### Easter eggs in the sunshine

The finished eggs look lovely on a bunch of winter honey-suckle. If you persuade friends and family to try their hand at decorating their own eggs, you will have a unique record of your Easter holidays.

**Egg hunt in the daffodils**
Behind the old malt house in Kingston Bagpuize is a delightful garden with an abundance of daffodils which makes a perfect place for an Easter egg hunt. The spicy fragrance of the blooms is surprisingly strong and far superior to their less fortunate shop cousins for the simple reason that these garden daffodils have been allowed to grow and mature in their own good time.

## Eggs a-plenty

The notion of eggs as a symbol of fertility pre-dates Christianity and existed in many early civilisations as did the custom of decorating them. When the Christian Church adopted the egg to symbolise Christ's resurrection, eggs were banned during Lent, a practice some Christians still respect today. On Easter Sunday, the ban was lifted and eggs – both edible and decorative – made a festive return to the table.

**One a penny, two a penny**

Easter calls for hot cross buns. The cross is said to symbolise Christ's crucifixion but some people believe crossed buns date back as far as pagan times.

**Mango Pavlova**

In my kitchen, crème caramel and pavlova go hand in hand: yolks for the former and whites for the latter. In this way, nothing goes to waste.

*serves 6*
*4 egg whites*
*250 g castor sugar*
*1 tbsp cornflour*
*1 tsp white vinegar*
*300 ml whipping cream*
*1 mango, diced*

Beat the egg whites. Fold in the sugar until the mixture is stiff. Whisk in the cornflour and vinegar. Line a baking tray with greaseproof paper and form a circle of meringue approximately 20 cm in diameter. Make a small hollow in the middle for the filling and bake at 150° C for 1½ hrs. Leave to cool and remove the greaseproof paper.

Place on a serving dish. Whip the cream and fold in the mango cubes and spoon into the hollow.

| Crème Caramel | serves 6 |
|---|---|
| *150 g sugar* | *350 ml whole milk* |
| *6 tbsp water* | *350 ml condensed milk* |
| *8 egg yolks* | *whipping cream* |

Grease 6 ramekins. Mix sugar and water in a pan, heat gently and stir until dissolved. Cook to a rich caramel without stirring. Carefully add 1 tsp of boiling water and pour the caramel into the ramekins. Leave to set. Beat the egg yolks together. Add the condensed milk and fresh milk and mix well. Sieve the mixture into the ramekins, on top of the caramel. Place in an ovenproof dish filled with 2 cm of water. Bake at 140° C for 45 mins until set. When cool, turn out on to a plate. Serve with whipped cream.

*Delicious desserts for Easter*

### Mother-of-pearl tiles

The shimmer of mother-of-pearl can be set off to great effect on tiles. The mould here is a wooden frame attached to a board with a removable cross at the centre. Take some ordinary cement and mix it with a little white cement to lighten the colour. Oil the board and pour in the cement. Leave for 10 mins, smooth the surface with a trowel and press in the shells. Allow to dry completely, remove the cross and you have your very own handmade tiles.

**Ammonite above the door**

This fossilised shell of an ammonite lends great character to the wall. Ammonites are often found in limestone, Oxfordshire's local stone. An ammonite can grow up to 2 metres in diameter, so this little fellow is a rather timid example.

**Swan mussels along the riverbank**

These shells are everywhere along the banks of the River Thames. Sometimes they even end up deep in nearby gardens, carelessly deposited by birds after a tasty meal. A thriving mussel population is a good sign of a clean river.

### Come rain, hail or shine

A few rays of sunshine are all
it takes to tempt the English
to lunch outdoors. Should sun
turn to rain, this is usually
taken with admirable stoicism.
I remember one summer's
day sitting at the outdoor
restaurant at Kenwood House
next to Hampstead Heath when
the weather suddenly changed
and rain started to fall. Utterly
unperturbed, everyone carried
on eating regardless of the
raindrops plopping on to their
plates. Anyway, there was little
they could do.

### Trout fishing

In early morning, anglers descend on to the riverbank to select the best spot for the day. Armed with fishing tackle and a bite to eat, they settle down to catch rainbow trout, salmon, pike or any of the other twenty species of fish in the Thames.

### The River Thames

The river is cleaner than it has been for years, and attracts a variety of wildlife. The kingfisher has returned, and even otters have been sighted – along with intrepid summer bathers.

### Barbecued rainbow trout

What is it about a barbecue that brings out the culinary instinct in all men? This trout dish is the creation of an occasional, but excellent, chef and should be prepared without too much regard for weighing and measuring. Clean a good sized trout (one per person). Stuff it with a handful of small shrimps and thinly cut slices of lime or lemon. Season with salt and pepper. Place the fish on a piece of foil; cover it with more slices of lemon and knobs of butter. Sprinkle with parsley. Wrap the fish in the foil and barbecue until tender (or bake in the oven at 220° C for 25–30 mins).

### Tulips in the greenhouse

The vinery (right) owes its name to a mature vine which covers most of the glass roof. The vine yields plenty of small, sweet grapes in the summer and a discreet layer of stickiness all year round. The old pulley system on the wall behind the table controls the roof windows allowing for good ventilation for all the plants. The pink tulips in the earthenware pot, the Tulip Ollioules, thrive in these conditions and because they are potted, they will last a lot longer. If you cover the soil with a bit of moss, it looks most attractive.

### Tulip Mania in Holland – or when the bubble burst

The history of the tulip is as colourful as the flower. Its name is a delightful corruption of the Persian word *dulband* meaning turban. Introduced to Holland from Constantinople in the 17th century, tulips soon became highly prized and bulbs an expensive commodity traded on the stock exchange. They sold at ever rising prices with one single bulb known to have fetched an astonishing 5000 guilders. Then, in 1637, the bubble burst, sending the Dutch economy into freefall in what was the world's first known stock market crash.

### From tulips to tote bag

Bathed in sunlight, the luminous quality of these tulips provided the inspiration for some water colour painting. This was then transformed into a simple tulip design and ended up as a decoration for this tote bag. Here is how: scan in the painted image and print out onto a T-shirt transfer sheet. Place the transfer on to some pale fabric and iron on according to instructions. The transfer print will make the fabric slightly stiff which will help to reinforce the bag. Sew the material into a simple tote bag with the lining and handle in matching fabrics.

### Kingston Bagpuize House

Well shielded from the main road lies this manor house from 1660. Redesigned some fifty years later during the reign of Queen Anne, it remains a private home, but is open to the public on certain days of the year.

### An old estate

Behind the weathered walls of the garden are the old outbuildings. Their names bear witness to their original function, The Old School House, The Malt House, and The Granary.

### Mr Bachepuis is still here

The site of Kingston Bagpuize is much older than the present house. In 1066, the property was seized from the Saxons and leased to the Norman Ralf de Bachepuis whose name endures to this day.

## China at Kingston Bagpuize House

The 'famille-verte' enamelled porcelain vases on the mantelpiece date back to the Kangxi period (1662-1722). Chinese porcelain began to reach England in the 1500s. It was considered a magical material, the secrets of which were not discovered in Europe until the early 18th century. English porcelain first appeared in the 1740s, much of it decorated with fantastical chinoiseries including mythical dragons and other beasts in exotic landscapes.

## Chinoiserie in Europe

The whimsical mix of Chinese and European taste makes Chinoiserie so irresistible. The style developed on the back of Marco Polo's travels to the East which inspired a passion for all things Oriental. Craftsmen in Europe soon began producing exotic imagery 'in the Chinese style' (of which they rarely knew much) for ceramics, silks and furniture. The Chinese responded with 'Westernised' goods for export, and by the mid-18th century, this hybrid style reached its peak and remains a popular theme today.

### A Chinoiserie box

Inspired by the Chinoiserie at Kingston Bagpuize House, I embarked on a small Chinoiserie project of my own (left). At a textile fair in Oxford, I found some exquisite scraps of fabric from a 1930's kimono. Although it was Japanese, the material reminded me of the Chinese wallpaper (opposite page) hanging in the hall at Kingston House which a member of the family brought back from China after World War II.

**Irresistible mini-spring rolls**  *makes approximately 40*

| | |
|---|---|
| *500 g minced pork* | *1 tbsp soy sauce* |
| *1 onion, finely chopped* | *1 tsp sesame oil* |
| *2 cloves of garlic, finely chopped* | *40 squares of spring roll pastry, 14 cm x 14 cm* |
| *1 tsp fresh root ginger, grated* | *1 beaten egg for sealing* |
| *1 carrot, finely chopped* | *oil for frying* |

Mix all ingredients and season. Allow to rest for 30 mins. Spoon some of the mixture onto a pastry square. Roll up, folding in the two sides as you go to form a 7 cm long roll. Seal with egg. Fry until golden brown. Serve with sweet chili sauce.

## A romantic folly

Tucked away in the garden of Kingston Bagpuize House lies a red brick folly; except this one is almost too useful to be known as such as follies were usually wholly nonsensical structures built solely to please the eccentricities of their owners.

When you enter, there is a narrow staircase leading up to a strangely formal room with wooden panelling and an old fireplace, suggesting that this was once intended as an outdoor banqueting room, not uncommon in the 18th century.

### The wedding dress

Vintage clothes make beautiful bridal outfits.

The laced bodice and cream skirt are from around 1910. The lacy scarf on top of the skirt is the only new garment in the ensemble. The parasol is from the 1880s in Honiton lace. The shoes are from around 1925 and the small handbag, with handmade tassels and embroidery in Chinese silk, dates from 1820–40. Most of these items come from fairs and antique shops in and around Oxford.

### Lace bowl for sugared almonds

This lace bowl (right) can be made in no time. Use a fabric doily with lace edges and immerse it thoroughly in a thick, creamy mixture of pva glue and water. Choose a small bowl or beaker as a mould and cover in cling film. Turn your mould upside down and arrange the saturated doily on it. If the edges of the doily are too long to hang loose, pop the whole thing on top of a bottle or similar. Leave to dry in this position. Remove only when bone dry.

### Lace at a price

Lace is delicate and refined but life as a lace maker was anything but. Although the industry employed men, women and children, the main work force consisted of girls between the ages of 17 and 25. Beyond that age their eyes could no longer take the strain. Honiton in Devon is famous for its lace of exquisite quality with production only having ceased in the middle of the twentieth century. Made with a very fine thread, Honiton lace is highly sought after, particularly in Japan and other countries of the Far East.

### Antique textile fairs

The English fan (left) dates from around 1875. I found it at one of the many antique textile fairs which specialise in antique fabric, clothes and haberdashery. To my eternal puzzlement, antique textiles are very much cheaper than other antiques, so you can usually strike a good bargain.

### Sugared lace for the wedding

When it comes to cake decoration – or any other culinary expertise for that matter – Ami Ciborowski is a true artist and the *masterchef* behind most dishes in this book.

### St Michaels and All Angels

This fine church in Clifton Hampden sits high up on the banks of the River Thames. Dating from the 13th century, it underwent a major transformation in the 19th century spearheaded by the architect Sir Gilbert Scott. He described his work as a 'refoundation' because, as he explained, 'there was hardly anything left to restore'.

### Wedding presents in lace

Old net curtains can be put to good use as gift wrapping. Dip in ink or dye or use some tea or coffee to give a soft, creamy hue.

### Bridesmaid's posy

The bridesmaid's posy is kept simple with pale peachy roses and Lily of the Valley. Leaves from the Lily of the Valley support the arrangement, which is tied with a wide lace ribbon.

Historically, the number of bridesmaids reflected the importance of the family. Dressed in white like the wife-to-be, they also helped to confuse any lurking witches.

### White wedding flowers

The big white snowballs from
the shrub, *Vibernum opulus
roseum*, make splendid wedding
decorations.

The embodiment of
romance, the Lily of the Valley
is the traditional wedding
favourite. It is petite, white
and delicate, has the sweetest
fragrance and flowers in May.
That it is also poisonous and
has been used as heart
medicine are facts best not
discussed here.

### Not for the faint-hearted

The three-tiered wedding
cake has its origins in Victorian
England when only the bottom
tier was edible. The rest was
decoration made from spun
sugar or paper. These days, the
entire cake is edible, although
not necessarily on the day of
the wedding. That the top tier,
the Christening cake, is often
saved for the christening
celebrations of the first child
came as a bit of a surprise to
me when my English friend
presented me with a two year-
old slice of cake – but it did
have fresh icing.

### For better, for worse

How did honeymoon
acquire its peculiar name?
There are many fanciful
explanations, but the
following two theories seem
the most convincing: that it
derives from a fermented
honey drink called mead,
which the bride was given in
the first month of marriage
to boost her fertility and
secure a male heir. The
other is that it refers to the
lamentably short month in
which the happy couple are,
indeed, happy!

### White on white

The *Small white* blends in perfectly with the sweet rocket and it is hard to say where the butterfly ends and the flower begins. The butterfly is attracted to the violet-like scent which grows stronger at night.

### Irises in the garden

Irises begin life strangely flat. The stem and leaves are almost two dimensional as if they had been cut out of green cardboard. Then they suddenly burst open and reveal a fluffy cloud of purple.

### With sketchbook in hand

Many people claim that they are useless at drawing. And this is before they have even tried. But as Betty Edwards, my favourite writer on drawing, explains in 'Drawing on the Right Side of the Brain', everybody can do so. The first step is to switch off that inner voice that constantly criticises every little pencil stroke. Only when the mind is a blank canvas, can you can finally begin to fully take in what you observe. This is a real challenge because the brain is so used to translating every impression. Drawing what you *actually* see takes a lot of practice.

## Irises on the table

The vivid purple of the irises creates a natural focal point on the table. The arrangement is deliberately kept low to enable the guests to see each other. As this particular silver dish is not suitable for flowers, I placed a glass bowl inside to hold the wet oasis. To provide the heavy stems with extra support, I took some chicken wire, shaped it into a dome and eased it over the oasis to hold the flowers securely. A small butterfly provided the finishing touch.

## The noble art of table laying

Table laying is much the same from country to country, but there are subtle differences. In England, the dessert spoon and fork can sometimes be placed alongside the plate as here. The French like to place their best silver forks with tines downwards – particularly if there are family monograms on the handle.

## Butterflies with beauty spots

This 19th century dinner service is Danish and designed by Jens Wilhelm Dahlerup, a distinguished architect of his day. Dahlerup also designed the Pantomime Theatre in Tivoli Gardens as well as other fine buildings in the Danish capital.

The Butterfly pattern first appeared in Denmark in the 1870s. Ironically, in its day, this decorative pattern was not as sought-after as simple white dinner plates edged with a thin, coloured line. In fact, the Butterfly pattern made a virtue out of necessity by concealing any imperfections that might have occurred during production, the rustic vine trellis border conveniently masking any flaws on the rim.

### The study of a butterfly

The Butterfly dinner service came in two versions, one of a superior quality, and a cheaper version for everyday use. With the latter, the butterflies were painted without too much regard for anatomical accuracy.

In the finer version, as on the plate above, the butterflies were truer to nature and painted with a more refined hand.

### A lady's posy

In the 19th century, it was fashionable for young ladies to fasten a posy to their dress or hair. The posy holder was often made of silver or porcelain and could be highly elaborate. The posy would usually have a rose in the middle, with smaller flowers around it. Dahlias were also popular, but if you wanted to use the secret language of flowers, the way to signal love was with a red rose. A yellow one merely meant friendship.

### Unpretentious flowers

Small vases are handy for the stems left over from more elaborate arrangements. They need not be proper vases, in fact most of these glass containers are perfume bottles picked up for a few pennies at a local car boot sale.

### Spring in the round window

The window is full of pretty meadow flowers: from top left they are Bigroot Geranium, Meadow Rue and Columbine with its lovely nickname Granny's Bonnet. The lower shelf has cornflower, Bigroot Geranium, Mourning Widow and lilac.

## Wisteria from the East

Chinese Wisteria, *Wisteria sinensis*, arrived in England in 1816 and rapidly gained popularity as 'the foremost of all climbing plants introduced into Europe.' Keen wisteria growers, the Japanese exported their version to England in the 1830s where it gradually took over from the Chinese variety. Should you be in doubt as to its origin, nature has so designed it that the Japanese wisteria curls clockwise while its Chinese cousin grows anti-clockwise.

## Fragile blooms

The wisteria on the left has grown to almost the same size as the one on the right, which is more than one hundred years older. Both are Chinese, just like the wisteria 'tree' in the middle. Pretty as they are, the cut blooms never last long – not in water and certainly not out of it. I had to work rather fast to try to capture them in a sketch before they wilted.

## Floral filing

A workspace becomes much more inviting if you decorate the spines of indispensable box files with attractive pictures. Choosing images that match the content also provides for easy reference. Since these files (right) contained material on the seasons, I chose pictures that corresponded to the time of year. As I needed three files for each season, I measured the height and width of one spine and multiplied the width by three. I enlarged my photograph to fit across three spines and printed it on good quality paper. I then cut the image into three (one for each spine) so that the sections formed a whole when placed side by side. Finally, I spray glued the pictures on to the files.

### Nature's fast food

You don't need to be an expert
to grow rhubarb. It is hardy,
beautiful and ripens as early as
May – ready to be pulled by
hand. Couldn't be simpler.

**Rhubarb and almond crumble from Waddesdon Manor**   *serves 6*

We indulged in this delicious pudding whilst soaking up the first rays of spring sun on the terrace of one of Waddesdon Manor's restaurants. Situated near Aylesbury, the 19th century renaissance-style chateau boasts exquisite interiors and gardens. Here is the rhubarb crumble, courtesy of the chef.

| Fruit compote: | Topping: |
|---|---|
| *1 kg rhubarb, chopped* | *100 – 150 g castor sugar* |
| *100 g castor sugar* | *125 g plain flour* |
| | *100 g ground almonds and some flaked almonds* |
| | *100 g butter (room temperature)* |

For the compote: wash and cut the unpeeled rhubarb into 2 cm pieces. Bake at 180° C for 10 mins or until just soft. Add 100 g castor sugar (or to taste). Leave to cool and place in ramekins. Cover with the topping.

For the topping: mix sugar, flour and ground almonds together. Cut the butter into small pieces, rub into the crumble mixture and spoon on top of the rhubarb. Sprinkle with flaked almonds and bake in a hot oven until the rhubarb is baked through. Serve with custard or cream.

### Pretty to behold today – but...

An 1880 survey from Clifton Hampden states: 'Cottage no 1: 8 children and only 2 very small bedrooms. Cottage no 29: front of house falling out, very damp house, 5 children, nice people. Cottage no 58: house very bad indeed, wife dead, 6 children, 2 at work, man has been great drunkard. Cottage no 35: room useless from damp, smoke very bad, 5 boys at home, only 2 bedrooms, good nice people. Cottage no 33: thatch very bad, ignorant people, never come to church'.

### Sweet lilac

As children, we would pick lilacs on our way home from school and suck out the honey from the small stems. I have to admit I still do this now and again. You can even mix entire flower heads into a salad if you are so inclined.

### The English garden

There is something very special about old English cottage gardens. Abundant, but not overgrown, well-tended but not contrived. Their charm lies precisely in their cheerfulness and lack of pretension. Modest bluebells grow alongside rare old roses, and both are lovingly tended. As the gardening expert Margery Fish said, 'always gay and never garish, and so obviously loved'.

### Glorious gardens

May is the time to fill the house with bunches of fragrant lilacs, star-shaped wild hyacinths, *Camassia leichtlinii*, and the wonderfully scented *Rosa rugosas*.

### Flowers by the pump

Once the flowers have had a good drink they are ready to be arranged. Most flowers benefit from a half hour in tepid water, ideally with a little floral preservative. Lilacs prefer an even longer soak.

### The seven golden rules of flowers

– Pick flowers in the early morning when they are full of sap.

– Use a sharp knife, not scissors, and for thicker branches use secateurs.

– Cut the stems at an angle so that the surface area takes up more water.

– Remove the leaves from the lower part of the stems, otherwise they will rot.

– Cut away unopened buds as they steal too much nourishment from the rest.

– Add a drop of bleach and a little sugar to keep the water fresh.

– Change the water in the vase every other day.

## Birds and feathers

The hummingbird wallpaper (facing page) is of contemporary design by Cole & Son. Birds have always been a popular design feature, and feathers have been used in everything from lampshades to these handcrafted tassels.

## Panoramic wallpapers

The wallpaper above is from Kingston Bagpuize House (see also p.32). Bought in China some sixty years ago, this panoramic wallpaper forms one continuous scene with no repeat pattern. Europe, and France in particular, had its own production of scenic wallpapers in the 19th century and today a few companies, such as de Gournay and Zuber, still produce them using their original designs. These were often scenes of far-flung places with exotic folklore and scant regard for geographical accuracy. Zuber uses its original hand-carved wood blocks to print its designs, such as Hindustan (from 1807), Eldorado (from 1840) and many more. A full scene might require up to twenty panels, 1,700 wood blocks and more than 200 colours. Small wonder that scenic wallpaper has become a collector's item.

### Bird in a golden cage

Popular since the 18th century, bird cages became particularly fashionable in Victorian times. Sometimes the cage contained a mechanical bird which would sing to order.

### The last flowers of spring

For this arrangement I mixed lilac with pink bistorta, *Rosa rugosa* and scarlet peonies from the garden. The flowers look lovely together and their perfume easily fills a whole room.

# The spirit of summer

Summer is more than a season; it is a state of mind, a collection of impressions. A dried flower for a book mark. A leisurely trip in a canoe. Warm evenings spent outdoors watching the sun go down and the sense of time stretching out before you.

# Roses

You love the roses – so do I. I wish

The sky would rain down roses, as they rain

From off the shaken bush. Why will it not?

Then all the valley would be pink and white

And soft to tread on. They would fall as light

As feathers, smelling sweet; and it would be

Like sleeping and like waking, all at once!

George Eliot
(1819–1880)

**The fishpond at Quat' Saisons**

The fishpond is tranquillity itself, but for centuries it served as a larder providing ducks and fish for the dinner table at Great Milton Manor. Today that table has been transformed into a gourmet restaurant and the manor is better known as the hotel Le Manoir aux Quat' Saisons. Its two Michelin-starred restaurant is run by Raymond Blanc, the world famous chef, who manages to combine *haute cuisine* with a relaxed and cheerful atmosphere.

**A rose walk for all weathers**

The rose walk was well established when we took over this garden (right). The lovely Rose Blush Ramblers cover the arches and we soon learned that this fragile looking rose is able to withstand a sudden gust better than most other roses.

**From purple to blue**

Nursing mothers are said to benefit from tea brewed from purple Goat's Rue or *Galega officinalis* (far left). Erect and proud, it stands almost as tall as the dainty sweet pea, *Lathyrus odoratus* (middle). But there is no such fragrance from California lilac (right) as this fluffy blue *Ceanothus* has no scent whatsoever. Californian settlers were merely struck by its resemblance to its sweet-scented cousin back home.

### Garsington Manor

Perched high on green hills, Garsington Manor holds a commanding view of the countryside. In 1915, the 17th century manor was restored by its then owners, Philip and Ottoline Morrell, who turned it into a lively meeting place for members of the Bloomsbury Group, including the writers Virginia Wolf and E. M. Forster. For the past twenty years, it has formed the picturesque backdrop to Garsington Opera founded by the late Leonard Ingrams and his wife Rosalind.

### The opera singers

With just 500 seats, the intimate atmosphere of Garsington Opera has succeeded in attracting outstanding artists. The scene on the right is from Mozart's *Cosi fan tutte*.

### Theatrical setting

The elevated terrace has been cleverly transformed into a stage and the three-arched loggia provides a dramatic setting. Both were added by the Morrells who also created an Italian garden which can still be enjoyed today.

### Self-service with style

Although there is excellent food on offer, guests are welcome to bring their own picnic hampers and relax in the gardens. And so they do – with a glass of champagne under the old copper beech.

**Cream tea at Garsington**

Delicious cream teas are unpacked and stylishly laid out next to the fish pond. The pond was converted into a pool in the early 1920s by the Morrells, who made it the focus of their new Italianate garden: 'We have run amuck and bought some statues in the desire to make Garsington more Italian'.

| **Mini-éclairs** | *makes 20–30* | |
|---|---|---|
| *150 ml water* | *pinch of salt* | Glacé icing: |
| *50 g butter* | *2 eggs, lightly beaten* | *100 g icing sugar* |
| *65 g plain flour* | *Filling: 250 ml double cream* | *1–2 tbsp water* |

Boil water and butter in a saucepan, add the flour and salt and beat vigorously until the dough comes away from the sides of the pan. Remove from the heat and allow to cool slightly. Add the eggs gradually, beating well. With a forcing bag (2.5 cm nozzle) pipe out dough into 5 cm lengths on to a greased baking tray. Bake at 200° C for around 15 mins until golden. When cool, split the éclairs down one side and fill with whipped cream. Decorate with glacé icing.

## Scones

*makes about 15*

*375 g plain flour*

*1½ tsp bicarbonate of soda*

*½ tsp salt*

*90 g unsalted butter, diced*

*3 tbsp sugar*

*1 egg, slightly beaten*

*300 ml milk*

*2 tbsp buttermilk*

For serving:

*clotted cream (or double cream), jam*

Method:

Sift flour, baking powder and salt into a bowl. Rub the butter into the mixture until it resembles breadcrumbs. Add sugar and make a hollow in the dough. Beat the egg and milk together and pour into the hollow. Mix the dough until it comes together, place on a floured surface and knead lightly. Roll out to a thickness of 2 cm and cut out the scones with a 5 cm pastry cutter. Place on a floured baking tray, brush with milk. Bake at 220° C for approximately 15 mins until golden. Enjoy warm with clotted (or whipped) cream and jam.

## Laburnum's golden chain

Summer has arrived when the laburnum is in bloom. The *Laburnum x wateri Vosii* graces the pond at Garsington Manor where its yellow blossoms spread a golden canopy over an old Italian statue. The beauty of the sight belies the highly poisonous seeds.

The clusters of blossoms are known as 'golden chains'. As they hang there in all their splendour, they look like shining lights, which gave me the idea for the garden lantern.

## A golden lantern

You need large golden beads; small, green glass beads; thick and thin gold wire; a gold-sprayed metal base, e.g. from an old lantern.

Form a spiral core by winding some thick wire round a pencil or the like. Take a long piece of thin wire (you will need many pieces). Thread the first gold bead on to it, twist a stalk of 2 cm and wind on to the spiral. Continue like this, adding the odd green bead here and there. Form two more chains of different lengths. Attach the three chains to the base. Suspend the lantern from beaded wire.

### Water lilies in the pond

The white water lilies flower from the end of May till September when it turns chilly again. Lilies are a real delicacy for carp but ours don't seem to know that so both thrive happily in our pond.

### Floating beauty

Fragrant white erigerons float next to yellow Roses of Sharon, known by the less romantically inclined as Aaron's Beard because of their prominent tufts.

### Swans on the Thames

There is a silent grace to the Mute Swan (*Cygnus olor*) as it floats down the river. Despite its name, it will hiss loudly if upset – which might just be the case come July when all the swans are counted in the local annual Swan Upping ceremony.

# To sit in the shade on a fine day

### Deceptive buttercups

Early June is a profusion of yellow. The intense colour of the rape fields gives way to a cascade of cheerful buttercups. Foul tasting and poisonous, they have every reason to rejoice as no horse or cow will go near them unless driven by starvation.

### Out of a fairy tale

Tucked away among lush greenery lies this enchanting cottage, which looks as natural in the landscape as if it had grown out of the soil itself. It is but one of the countless cottages dotted along the Thames, the charms of which never cease to delight me.

**Artichokes as aphrodisiac**

Artichokes were grown by the Greeks and Romans long before they were introduced into Northern Europe in the 1500s. The proud looking vegetable was a favourite of Henry VIII, who may have been as attracted by its perceived aphrodisiac qualities as by its taste.

Artichoke bottoms are a real delicacy. Boil them in salted water for about 30 mins, making sure they are fully immersed or they will turn brown. Serve the the artichokes warm with butter or vinaigrette.

**Vegetables in abundance**

According to Terry Johnson (above), our knowledgeable gardener, lettuce can be sown throughout spring and summer, a little at a time. The same goes for radishes and spring onions.

**Straight and neat**

Terry has a great knack for salvaging old garden tools. This metal garden line is in constant use and ensures that the rows, or *drills* as he would have it, remain straight and neat.

### The beauty of vegetables

This is one of my favourite work spaces as the light from the glass roof makes it ideal for drawing.

Vegetables are fun to draw, but are often overlooked in favour of flowers. That's a real shame as many vegetables are every bit as beautiful. An ordinary cabbage – or even a lettuce – has so much texture and colour. Or take a look at the underside of a mushroom. There's a real challenge.

### Vegetables in the vase

Rhubarb leaves (right) make excellent 'vase-fillers' and provide a dramatic setting for purple blossoms such as the lupins and alliums arranged in this green vase. Footballs, as the big, round Alliums are called in our garden, are also known as ornamental onions. They are a cross between a flower and a vegetable and come in many colours and varieties. The Star of Persia, or *Allium christophii*, is the largest, with flower heads of up to 25 cm in diameter.

### From Sweden with love

The British love affair with the Aga is one of the few constants in life. This green Aga, however, belongs to a Swedish family, but then it was a Nobel-prize winning Swede, Gustaf Dalén, who first invented the Aga in 1929. Cooking Aga-style can seem rather bewildering to the uninitiated. If you use the oven, the hobs get colder, and stir-frying is totally out of the question. Still, it looks homely, keeps the kitchen warm and makes an unbeatable Sunday roast.

### Vegetables on the tablemats

Personalised tablemats are easy to make. For the vegetable mats above, either use photographs or place real vegetables directly on to a scanner. Using a graphic computer programme, adjust the colours and size. Print the design on to a T-shirt transfer sheet and iron on to strong, white fabric. Remember to invert the image on the computer so it reproduces correctly on the fabric, particularly if you have text in the design. Cut the table mat to size. The plastic-like finish of the transfer print will prevent the cloth from fraying.

## Daisy, daisy...

The daisy is said to have derived its name from 'day's eye' because of the way it opens up its whole head in the morning and closes it again at night. As any child will tell you, daisies make pretty chains (right) but in case your daisy chain skills are a bit rusty, here is how: with a fingernail, pierce a hole towards the end of the stem. Pull the next daisy through the hole. Go on like this till you have a chain. For a garland, close the loop by threading the entire head of the first flower through it.

## Pimm's in the garden

Before moving to England I had never come across Pimm's but after twenty years in this country I find it inextricably linked to warm summer evenings in the garden. Here is one way of making it: Pimm's No 1 and a fizzy drink or sparkling mineral water (1 part Pimm's to 3 parts soft drink). Add a few cucumber slices, mint leaves and a small flower for decoration.

Personally, I prefer a bubblier, less sweet version: mix 1 part Pimm's No 1 with 3 parts champagne.

### Mme du Barry on the folder

The folder on the table is decorated with a portrait of Mme du Barry, the mistress of Louis XV who survived the king, but was guillotined in 1793 during the Reign of Terror.

To make the folder, transfer your pictures to a computer and print on to a T-shirt transfer sheet. With a scalpel, cut out the motifs from the sheet and iron on to a piece of white fabric large enough to cover a folder. Frame the portrait with lace ribbon. Spray glue the fabric on to the folder, folding the raw edges over the inside. Line this with pretty wallpaper. Sew on two ribbons.

### Toile de Jouy

The walls are decorated in *Toile de Jouy*. The wallpaper takes its name from the French town of Jouy-en-Josa, home of the Oberkampf print factory which produced some of the finest toile designs from 1760–1843. The toiles typically depict people in pastoral scenes, in red or blue monochrome against a light background. The factory survived the French Revolution and subtly adjusted its designs by replacing royalty with citizens to reflect the new political climate.

### Climbing roses

The window opens out to the perfume of roses. Unable to support their own weight, the climbers are secured to the wall, but in nature they use their thorns to help with their climbing.

### The secret language of fans

Fans were once an essential accessory in polite society. This fan from around 1750 has a typical rococo motif of aristocratic couples in a pastoral setting.

A sophisticated language developed around the fan over the years: a fan in the lady's right hand in front of her face indicated 'follow me'. A half-open fan pressed against her lips invited a kiss. But if the lady twirled her fan in her right hand, her heart was otherwise engaged.

### Rococo flowers

Between 1720–50, fashion was characterised by large floral patterns and bold colours in the spirit of rococo, or *Louis Quinze*, as the French prefer. The rococo style, with its mussel shells, scrolls and grottos, was highly ornamental and full of *joie de vivre*. The embroidery on the gown (right) reflects the new trend for smaller floral motifs which began to emerge in the 1760s. With its large, red *Paeonia officinalis rosea plena* and the small, white Evening Stars, the arrangement above reflects both styles.

**Dress for a tiny waist**

To me, antique costumes
are living, breathing history.
This Scottish *contouche*, or
*robe à la française,* in em-
broidered silk dates from
the 1760s. It is of diminutive
size and consists of a petti-
coat, a stomacher and a
robe. The robe is a so-called
sack back with elegant
*Watteau* folds from neck to
floor. The original stomacher
is lost, probably because
this was a loose item which
had to be sewn on every
time the gown was worn.

**The art of *trompe l'oeil***
The Garden Hall has fine wood panels beneath the windows, but on the other walls they are an illusion created by a paint brush. Ironically, what was once a paltry imitation has now become an art form.

**Gooseberry Fool**     *serves 6–8*
Gooseberries make a delicious fool. If the berries are too tart, add some *crème anglaise* to sweeten.

Fool:
*500 g gooseberries*
*2 tbsp elderberry cordial*
*3½ tbsp sugar (or to taste)*
*150 ml whipping cream*

Top and tail the gooseberries. Put in a saucepan and simmer at low heat. Stir until the juice begins to run. Slowly increase the heat to just below boiling point and simmer for a further 5 mins until the berries have softened. Add the elderberry cordial and sugar to taste. Leave to cool. Mash the larger fruit pieces with a fork. Fold in the whipped cream. Serve like this or sweeten with a *crème anglaise*.

Crème anglaise:
*150 ml single cream*
*3 egg yolks*
*2 tsp cornflour*
*1 tbsp castor sugar*

Beat the egg yolks with the cornflour and sugar. Heat the cream until it begins to boil, remove from the heat and add to the egg mixture while stirring vigorously. Return the crème anglaise to the pan and reheat carefully to thicken. Leave to cool. Add to the gooseberry fool.

### Wine in the Vinery

The vinery (right) is an enchanting hideaway. The branches of the vine have spread like tentacles covering the walls and ceiling. It yields some fine sweet grapes in late summer.

### Gold leaf decoration

Gilding need not be costly if you use so-called leaf metal sheets as I did for this glass dish. They come in gold, silver and copper and can be applied to a smooth surface or, as in this case, brushed on to to a slightly coarser texture (which conveniently hides the odd, unintentional crease). You need glue, a brush, a cloth and a steady hand for the flimsy sheets. Then simply follow the instructions on the pack. I gilded this dish on the underside only and finished off with two coats of varnish to protect it from scratches.

**The rose garden**
Surrounded by old-fashioned English roses, the table is laid for a sparkling summer lunch.

**Empire versus Regency**
The champagne glasses are from around 1810–20 in French Empire, a style highly influenced by Napoleon's Egyptian campaign.

Regency, the equivalent English style, (circa 1800-1830), also followed this trend but with markedly less military zeal.

### A rose for every guest

For special occasions, these silk pomanders make great table decorations and can be filled with a small gift or a piece of cake. I have to admit I bought mine ready-made, but they are easy to make. With pinking shears, cut a 40 cm circle from silk fabric. Fold over a 4 cm seam along the edge, iron the fold. Sew a running thread of elastic 3 cm from the fold. Pull the thread loosely together to create a draw-string. Secure the thread. Fill the pomander with goodies, tie a ribbon along the seam and top off with a silk flower or a fragrant rose.

### Old English roses

No English garden is complete
without roses. The British are
passionate gardeners and
have an unrivalled knack for
making everything look lovely
and deceptively effortless. I
particularly like what is referred
to on the Continent as an
'English garden'; a softer, flowing
design without formal beds or
strict, dividing borders.

### Silk dress with roses

This evening gown caught
my eye at an antique
textiles fair because of its
soft green colour and the
lovely silk and velour roses.
Designed by a certain
Louis Copé of Harrogate,
it dates from the 1950s,
the last decade of seriously
glamorous ball gowns.

### Roses from the garden

The gown provided the
inspiration for these cream
and soft pink silk flowers
on the right.

## The meaning of a rose

When I first moved to England I was surprised to learn that an English rose is not a rose at all, but a pretty young girl with a fair complexion.

Most cultures have their own specific 'rose-code'. Almost universally, the rose symbolises the soul and the red rose, in particular, represents purity and love. The rose can also refer to secrecy as in 'sub-rosa', which is said to originate from the ancient Romans. And in Scandinavia, in days gone by, a rose salon was not necessarily a room with roses but rather a room in which one was left undisturbed.

## Fabric flowers

*Materials*: various shades and colours of silk, chiffon or thin velvet; a little felt; sewing thread; 1 brooch clip. The roses measure 8-10 cm in diameter.

*The inner bud:* cut a 12-13 cm bias strip from the darkest shade and fold it lengthwise. Sew a running thread along the raw edge of the folded strip. Pull the running thread to create the inner rose bud by rolling it into a small spiral. When the rose bud has the right shape and size (roughly 1.5 cm in diameter) stitch together to secure. Cut a 4-5 cm circle of felt and stitch the rosebud to the middle. Now add the petals.

*Petals*: using the other colours, cut out 7 to 9 oval shapes (on the bias) in various sizes, from 10-20 cm long. Fold lengthwise into a crescent shape and sew a running thread along the curved edge. Pull the thread to fold the petal slightly. Place the smallest petals around the rosebud, making sure each one slightly overlaps. Stitch to the felt base. Continue with the larger pieces. *Leaves:* cut out 2 leaves; create 'veins' with large running stitches. *Assemble:* sew on to the brooch clip. To neaten, cover the base with a second felt base and cut holes for the clip. Sew on to the base.

### Hanging pretty

It takes no time to give a boring wooden hanger 'girl appeal'. All it needs is two coats of pink paint, a sticker or picture glued on to both sides and two coats of varnish to seal it all.

### A little doll's house

From Regency mansions to a two up, two down (right), Britain is foremost in doll's houses. The most exquisite example I have ever seen is Queen Mary's 1920s house at Windsor Castle.

### Dainty flowers

The Redleaf Rose (left) and other small flowers are a recurring theme in this room and are picked up in the curtains, bed linen and table cloth. The hand basin is a reminder of a time when bathrooms were scarce and certainly not en-suite.

# That which we call a rose

### Pink seaside daisies

These seaside daisies, or *Erigeron glaucus*, climbing our garden steps originate from America where, as their common name implies, they mainly grow along the coast. Seaside daisies have longer and thinner stems than ordinary daisies and their petals are a riot of purple, pink and white.

### Cup cakes
*makes 12 cup cakes*

200 g castor sugar

250 g butter, room temperature

2 large eggs

175 g self-raising flour and 1 tsp baking powder

2 tbsp milk

150 g icing sugar (or as much as desired)

Beat together the sugar and butter until smooth and fluffy. Add the eggs, one at a time, beating well. Add the dry ingredients and the milk. Spoon the mixture into cup cake cases and bake at 180° C for about 20 mins or until golden brown. Mix the icing sugar with water until smooth. Cover the cold cup cakes with icing.

### Royal icing for the birthday cake

The birthday cake is covered in a thick layer of royal icing and decorated with sugar roses. It takes a bit of practice to get the icing smooth, but it is worth the effort.

*4 egg whites*     *800-900 g icing sugar, sifted*

*1 tbsp lemon juice*     *1½ tsp glycerine, fruit colouring*

Whisk the egg whites with a spoon, or carefully with an electric mixer, until white. Over beating gives an uneven finish. Gradually add icing sugar and whisk with the spoon. When half the sugar has been added, beat in the lemon juice. Continue adding more icing sugar, beating well until the icing forms small peaks when lifted with a spoon. Add the glycerine to keep the icing soft. Mix in a little fruit colouring. Cover with cling film and let it rest for 24 hrs before coating the cake with a ½ - 1 cm thick layer.

## Clematis of import

The lovely Clematis Lasurstern (right) inspired this appliquéd cushion (far right).

Although clematis are indigenous to Britain, foreign imports over the past 500 years have boosted numbers to around 300 today. Enthusiasm for clematis reached an all time high in the 19th century with exotic species arriving from China and Japan. But then the flowers were struck down by 'clematis wilt' caused by a fungus. Not until after World War II were stocks fully replenished.

## The gazebo

Even the spindliest of gazebos is enough to give you a snug feeling of being cocooned in a room in the middle of the garden.

The word gazebo is popularly believed to derive from the verb to gaze although some argue that it has oriental roots owing to the fact that gazebos were introduced to Europe from China in the 18th century. At that time, demand for Chinese art and Chinoiserie was at its height and gazebos, along with romantic 'ruins' and other follies, quickly became the new must-have items for wealthy garden owners.

### Clematis cushion

The clematis are in appliqué of cotton, georgette and netting on a Thai silk cushion. Begin by drawing outlines of leaves on the reverse of the silk fabric. Machine stitch the outlines with 'free embroidery' setting. For each petal, cut out one base petal and two smaller pieces from different fabrics. Allow edges to fray. On the base petal, place the smaller pieces down the middle and machine embroider in place. Sew beads on to the 'stigma'.

### Frozen flowers

To add a dash of summer to ice-cubes freeze a small flower into each one. Use one of the many types of edible flowers such as pansies, borage, violets, lavender, carnations or hyacinths. Generally speaking, it is better to use the petals and not the receptacle.

Freeze the ice-cubes in two stages to prevent the petals from rising to the surface. Fill the ice-tray half way, add the flowers and freeze. When frozen, add the rest of the water. Boiled, distilled water makes the ice-cubes more transparent.

### Ice house by the river

Before the invention of the fridge, the ice house was a clever way of storing blocks of ice. Many ice houses were built in the 18th century as a sign of affluence. This ice house (left) dates from around 1850. It is atypical in that it is not dug into the ground, but built into a slope. Wrapped in straw and kept in the dark, the ice could last for years. It was cut from rivers and lakes and ice houses were a common sight along the Thames. Public ice houses were still selling large blocks of ice as recently as fifty years ago.

## Pink Sunrise

*½ shot vodka*    *Grenadine*
*tonic water*     *Bols/Curaçao*

Mix the grenadine and blue
Curaçao in a small jug. Pour
the vodka into a martini glass
and top up with tonic. Carefully
pour some of the grenadine
mixture into the glass, letting
it settle to the bottom. It will
slowly rise to the surface and
create what looks like a perfect
pink sunrise with spectacular
colours. Add ice cubes with
flowers frozen inside them
and decorate with pansies.

### Canoeing in the sun

The sun is out and the river comes to life. Narrow boats and canoes glide by at a leisurely pace, navigated with optimism and varying degrees of seamanship.

## Wrapped tuna

*serves 4*

*4 tortilla wraps* — *green lettuce, cleaned and washed*

*2 cans tuna in oil* — *1 small can of sweetcorn*

*mayonnaise to taste* — *1 red onion, thinly sliced*

Spoon a good layer of mayonnaise on the wrap, add some lettuce leaves, tuna, sweetcorn and sliced onion. Season with salt and pepper. Roll the wrap – enjoy.

## Marinated chicken drumsticks

*makes 20*

*20 chicken drumsticks* — *100 ml lemon juice*

*5 cloves of garlic, crushed* — *2 tbsp ketchup*

*4 tbsp clear honey* — *1 tsp black pepper*

*400 ml orange juice* — *2 tsp salt and 1 tsp soy sauce*

Mix all the ingredients for the marinade in a large bowl. Put the drumsticks into the bowl and cover well with the marinade. Put the bowl in the fridge for at least 4 hours or overnight. Roast the drumsticks on a roasting tray at 180° C for 30 – 40 mins. Delicious hot or cold.

I drank summer like a sweet wine

## An oasis in the garden

When the sun beats down, it provides shade. When it drizzles, it offers shelter. The pergola is an oasis in the garden. Here it is framed by clematis, sweet pea and roses. These sweet scented climbers are relatively quick to take hold whereas wisteria, vines and ivy take a little longer, but offer excellent shade. To stop birds from dropping unwelcome 'calling cards' from the roof, hammer a number of long nails halfway into the roof poles. Extend some string from nail to nail so that the birds can no longer perch there.

## Blue summer garden

Flowers look so lovely against blue glass. For this table (above), I used my collection of blue bottles for a simple arrangement of tall Maltese Cross and shorter stemmed *Rosa rugosa* .

To brighten up some old wooden garden chairs, I gave them a lick of blue paint and new backs and seats in a cheerful mix of fabrics. A simple makeover like this gives a fresh lease of life to the tiredest garden furniture, with little effort or expense.

### Raspberry ice-cream delights

*Serves 6*

The ice-cream:

*300 g raspberries*

*2 tbsp sugar and 2 tbsp water*

*4 tbsp icing sugar, sifted*

*3 egg yolks*

*400 ml double cream*

The sponge base:

*3 eggs*

*200 g sugar and 1 tsp vanilla sugar*

*125 g flour*

*1 tsp baking powder*

*¼ tsp salt*

*75 ml milk*

*6 pastry cutters:  4 cm high and*

*7.5 cm in diameter*

### The raspberry ice-cream

Make a purée by simmering the raspberries and sugar in 2 tbsp of water for 10 mins. Strain and put aside. Beat together icing sugar and eggs. Put aside. In a saucepan, bring half the cream to the boil and pour the egg and sugar mixture into this, beating briskly. When it thickens, remove from the heat. Allow to cool. Whip the remaining cream and fold into the egg mixture together with the raspberry purée. Freeze for 1 hour, then take out and stir well. Re-freeze for 30 – 45 mins.

### The sponge base

Beat eggs and sugar well. Add milk and vanilla sugar and beat lightly. Add flour, baking powder and salt. Bake on a small baking sheet at 180° C for 12 – 15 mins. Leave to cool.

### Assembly and serving

With the pastry cutters, cut out 6 cakes from the sponge base. Leaving the pastry cutters in place, pour the semi-frozen ice-cream on top of each cake and leave to freeze inside the cutters. Serve with mint leaves and raspberries or with a little raspberry purée.

# The spirit of autumn

Autumn has spread its golden mantel over the landscape and the Thames hastens its journey through beautiful Oxfordshire. With an almighty force it swells up and turns whole meadows into lakes in one majestic sweep.

# Ode to Autumn

Season of mists and mellow fruitfulness,

Close bosom-friend of the maturing sun;

Conspiring with him how to load and bless

With fruit the vines that round the thatch-eves run;

To bend with apples the moss'd cottage-trees,

And fill all fruit with ripeness to the core;

To swell the gourd, and plump the hazel shells

With a sweet kernel; to set budding more,

And still more, later flowers for the bees,

Until they think warm days will never cease;

For Summer has o'erbrimm'd their clammy cells.

John Keats
(1795–1821)

Association Kokopelli

For the Liberation of Seeds and Soil

Ripple Farm, Crundale, CT4 7EB. UK

## DWARF HARICOT BEAN
## FOR SHELLING
## < WHITE SOISSONS >

A very old variety with white beans.
Early and productive

*Phaseolus vulgaris*

Packet of approx 30g seeds
Year of harvest:2002 Viable life of seed 3 years

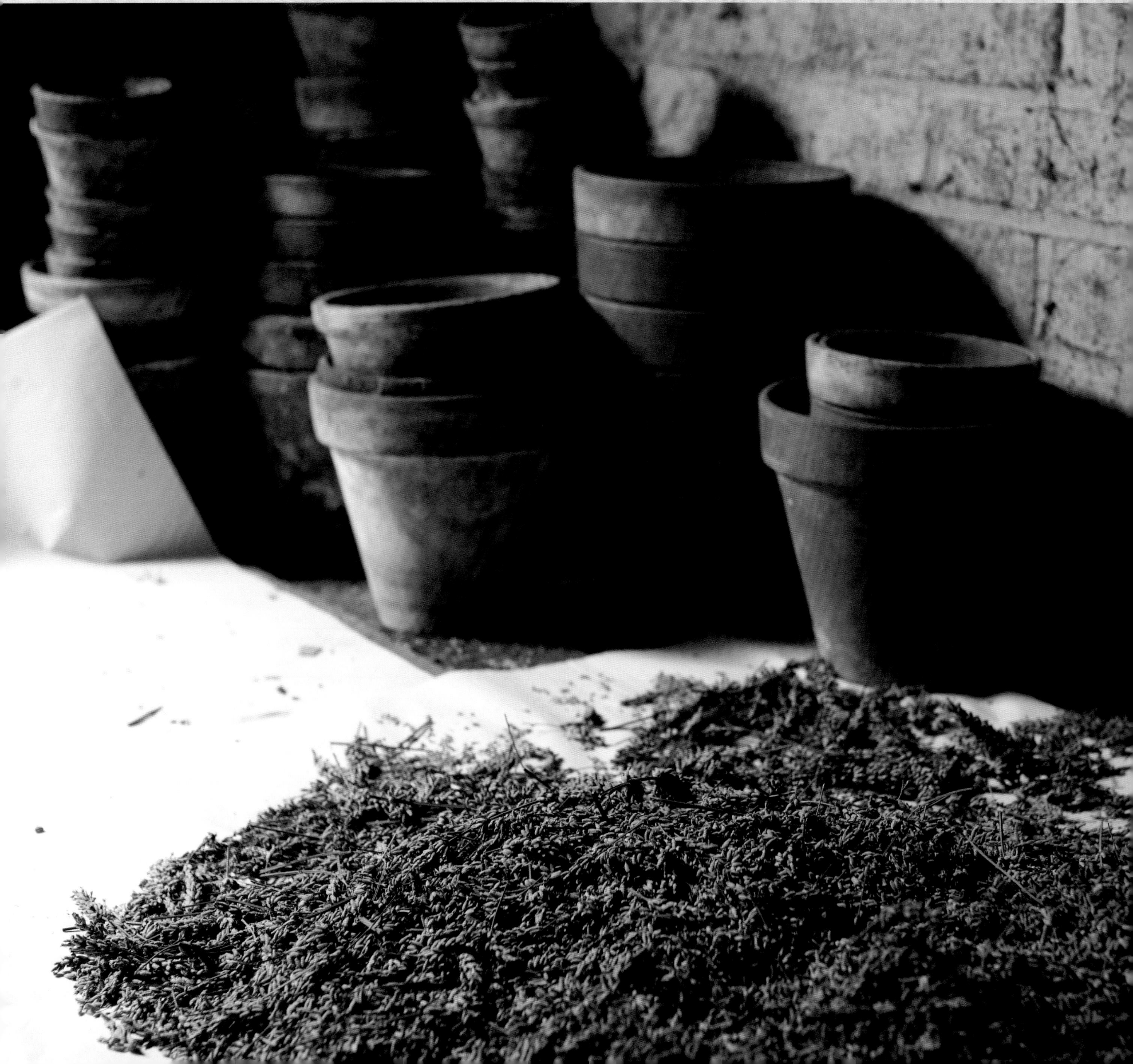

### The lavender fields of England

The scent of lavender is evocative of the warm days of summer. Although Provence is regarded as the home of lavender, the plant actually thrives as well, or even better, in the milder English climate. This is because during the hot Mediterranean summer, the scented flower oil tends to evaporate quicker than in England's cooler climes.

### The art of drying lavender

Picking lavender is all about timing. To catch the scent at its most powerful, the lavender should be cut just before pollination when the flowers are at their bluest and just about to bloom. Place the cut lavender in a warm dry place, and leave to dry completely for a couple of weeks. We once lost a whole summer's worth of lavender because we didn't leave it long enough. When dry, you can add a few drops of lavender oil, (preferably use pure essential oils as synthetic oils smell artificial). To prevent the oil from evaporating, mix it with a fixative like orris root powder. For a portion of 100 g of dried lavender, mix 5 tsp. orris root powder with 25 drops of lavender oil.

### Lavender bags

The German linen press (right) dates from the 1600s and the practice of scenting linen is just as old. Not only does lavender add fragrance, it is also said to improve your sleep and keep moths at bay.

Pretty lavender bags are easy to make if you have a few pieces of lace or crochet to spare. Make an inner pouch using a tightly woven fabric, like the pale lilac used here, and insert it into an outer bag of lace or crochet. Tie with a silk ribbon.

### Apple harvest

A fragrance of apples, onions and lavender greets you when you enter the apple store in the autumn. The apples are kept in strict order with each variety in its own place. Neatly laid out in rows on the shelves, no apple touches another so as to avoid spoiling the whole barrel. The apples will keep for an impressively long time in this dark, cool room. The Newton Wonder apples on the top shelf will last until March or April; the Cox Oranges are ready for Christmas. Other varieties, such as the eating apple, Beauty of Bath, should be enjoyed rather quickly.

### The apple picker bag

I admire the British talent for keeping traditional methods alive (even if it occasionally means choosing custom over comfort). Terry's apple picker bag (below) is a case in point. When full, instead of emptying the bag apple by apple or pouring them out in one go at the risk of bruising them, Terry simply unbuttons the sack allowing the apples to slide out unscathed. It is easier on the arms, but hard on the neck.

### Apple juice from the garden

If you have a garden full of apples but no time to cook them, forget about the puddings and the jellies, and simply make an honest jug of apple juice instead. It tastes better than the best juice money can buy, and it really doesn't take long to make. Peel and cut the apples, remove the cores and cut into small pieces ready for the juicer. Some apples are almost too rich in taste, in which case add a little water. The juice will easily keep for a couple of days in the fridge.

### Granny Kirsten's apple jelly

*1 kg chopped apples*
*water*
*1 kg sugar to 1 litre juice (or to taste)*
*vanilla pod*
*jelly bag or muslin and stand*
*sterilised, dry, warm jars*

Wash the apples and remove the stalks, but leave core and peel. Cut into small pieces, and put in a large saucepan. Add water to cover and simmer at low heat until the apples have softened.

Strain the apples through a jelly bag or use a muslin cloth suspended on an upturned stool as I do. Don't be tempted to squeeze out the last drops of juice as this will cloud the jelly. Measure the amount of strained juice. Pour into a thick-bottomed saucepan and add the required amount of sugar.

Remove the seeds from the vanilla pod and cut it into small pieces. Add pod and seeds to the juice. Boil slowly till the sugar has dissolved. Increase the heat and boil for a further 4–5 mins. The jelly is ready when the drops are heavy and sticky and a small amount remains on the spoon when you pour it. Let the jelly rest a few minutes then skim the surface with a slotted spoon. Pour into warm, sterilised jars. Allow to set and cool before adding a lid.

### Beetroot in sand

With beetroot you have to strike a balance to make sure they neither dry out nor become too moist. Stored in sand like this, they will keep for up to a couple of months.

### Borscht – Russian beetroot soup   *serves 8*

There are many variations of borscht, but this one is my friend Ami's special recipe and it is superb. Serve with freshly baked bread and ice-cold beer.

*5 beetroot*

*2 medium onions*

*3 celery sticks*

*2 medium cooking apples*

*1 red pepper*

*3 tbsp butter*

*3 tbsp olive oil*

*2½ litres stock*

*1 tsp dried thyme*

*1 bay leaf*

*freshly squeezed lemon juice*

*salt and freshly ground pepper*

*crème fraîche*

Peel and dice the vegetables. Lightly fry in butter and oil in a large saucepan. Add the stock, thyme and bay leaf. Cover and allow to simmer for approximately 30 mins, stirring occasionally. Mix in a food processor until smooth and creamy. Return the vegetables to the pan and add lemon juice to taste, salt and freshly ground pepper. Leave to simmer for a further 10 mins. Top each serving with a spoonful of crème fraîche.

### The apple store

I recall the first time I walked into this apple store. I couldn't believe my eyes – or nose, for that matter. The hoard of onions and shallots, boxes of beetroot in sand, carrots, potatoes and other root vegetables filled the room with an almost tangible smell, enriched with the perfume of drying lavender.

Every year, the strings of onions are the first produce to be stored here, soon followed by lavender, apples, pumpkins and the rest of the vegetables. Stored like this, everything lasts much longer and tastes a lot better.

### Glorious September

Autumn is my favourite season.
The trees are aflame with gold
and the smell of mulch and leaves
permeates the cooler air. To me,
this is the most inspiring time of
the year by far.

I have always enjoyed collecting
colourful leaves and nowadays my
children patiently indulge me in
this activity. They might even join
me in making an old-fashioned
herbarium, which is both visually
attractive and useful in my work as
a designer. Dried leaves look pretty
on greeting cards or as table
decorations.

Incense Rose

### An autumnal collection

Even if it has no immediate purpose, a cache such as this (left) fills me with a real feeling of abundance. The contents will always come in handy at some point.

The purple runner beans are highly decorative and the wooden 'buttons' can be used for all manner of things. Bark and cones complete the autumnal collection.

### A tree of many colours

Autumn has transformed the iron tree (right) into an explosion of orange-pink leaves which will last long after other trees have shed their foliage. Its wood is extraordinarily tough which is why it is known as the iron tree rather than the Latin *Parrotia persica*.

### Experimenting with autumn leaves

With some experimentation, all sorts of interesting print effects can be achieved without any special tools. For the dark blue design (below), I used water soluble dye, bleach, perforated paper and real leaves. To make the design, coat a sheet of good quality paper with dark blue, water soluble dye. Allow to dry. Dip the leaves in diluted bleach and place on the coated paper. The bleach will remove some of the dye, creating a diffuse image of the leaf in a lighter tone. Add texture by laying a perforated piece of paper on top of the blue background and dab with cloth soaked in bleach. Remember to wear gloves and a mask when using bleach, and preferably work outdoors.

### Happy accident

Good old serendipity was at work here (right page of sketchbook). I was designing an intricate leaf pattern, which involved dipping real leaves into blue dye, when I absent-mindedly dabbed the leaves on to some blotting paper to get rid of the excess dye. When I had finished my laborious project, I discovered that the blotting paper was much more attractive than the completed design.

## Disguised as spring

In mid-November, *Vibernum x bodnantense* (above) produces the most beautiful pink flowers reminiscent of early spring and it continues to bloom way into March. A hardy shrub, only a biting frost can kill the flowers, but they are quickly replaced by new ones. A couple of sprigs indoors will fill a room with the sweetest perfume. The splendid beauty-berries, *Callicarpa*, (left) also lend colour to the garden. If the shrub is protected from the cold, the berries will last until December or even January. They make very decorative flower arrangements and will easily keep for a couple of weeks without a single drop of water.

## Naked ladies

They look like overgrown crocuses, but are, in fact, Meadow Saffron, or *Colchicum autumnale* (right) and bloom in September–October. The bulbs can survive on a window sill without any soil or water, hence the nickname 'Naked Ladies'. Once planted, they'll go on flowering year after year. Meadow Saffron thrive in the sun or semi-shade. But take care, like so many other flowers they are as poisonous as they are pretty.

### The potting shed

There is an air of calm activity in the potting shed. Here are pots of every size, bags of seed and bulbs, riddles and tools, baskets, cans and old garden jottings.

This is where onions and bulbs are planted in flowerpots before being forced and where flowers are potted in eathenware pots ready to be taken indoors.

### Forcing hyacinth bulbs

The scent of hyacinths is so evocative of Christmas even though this is not their natural flowering season at all. To have them ready for the festive season, they have to be forced. Timing can be tricky though; we've had more than one Christmas when our hyacinths decided not to bloom until January. Plant pre-chilled hyacinth bulbs in a wide pot, with the necks of the bulbs above soil level. Place the pots in a dark, cool room for some two months. Water regularly to prevent the bulbs from drying out, then bring them into the warmth.

### Into the warmth

The hyacinths are ready to be brought indoors when the shoots begin to swell and reach a height of around 5 cm. Put the hyacinths in a warmish room (15°–18° C). Preferably, they should remain in the shade for the first two to three days to give them time to acclimatise. A few weeks later, the shoots will have grown into beautiful scented flowers.

### Vase with equine motif

Cotton balls on stems look warm and soft and last forever. To complement their texture, I made a vase from felt and added a blaze motif inspired by the horse above. With chestnut brown wool, I made a rectangular piece of felt, adding the white blaze down the front. When dry, I stitched it into a tube and eased it over a cardboard vase. I put some dried rice into the vase to stabilise the arrangement.

### Soft autumn cushions

For the cushions on the right, a horse's coat provided the inspiration once again, and was reflected in 'horsey-coloured' wool, mohair and suede. Before central heating, it was not unusual to change curtains every summer and winter. Such drastic measures are rarely needed today and a new set of cushions is usually enough to change the whole atmosphere of a room.

When the wind blows on a chilly autumn day, there is nothing like snuggling up to soft cushions with a cup of tea, some biscuits and a really good book.

### Auntie Elisabeth's biscuits    *makes about 60*

It wasn't easy to entice my sister-in-law to divulge the recipe for these delicious biscuits, but in the end she relented. It was worth the effort as these biscuits really do melt in the mouth.

*225 g slightly salted butter*          *100 g ground hazelnuts*
*85 g sugar*                            *200-225 g plain flour*

Method:

Beat the butter and sugar until completely smooth. Add the rest of the ingredients and mix well. Let the dough rest in the fridge for a couple of hours and then roll out into finger-width 'sausages'. Cut them into approximately 2.5 cm pieces and roll into balls. Grease a baking tray and dust with flour so that the biscuits are easy to remove after baking.

Arrange the biscuits on the baking tray and give each one a slight squeeze to form a kind of inverted boat shape (keel upwards, that is). Bake in the oven at 175-200° C for about 10 mins. Remove the biscuits from the baking tray while still hot.

### Crewel work

The cushions on this bed are in crewel work which is more common in British interiors than on the Continent. This form of embroidery, usually in worsted yarn on flax or linen, first emerged in Britain in the 17th century. It was specifically used for cushion covers, bedspreads and curtains. Today, the choice of fabric is not restricted to linen, as illustrated by this velour cushion on the left.

### Crewelled chinoiserie

Historically, crewel work designs were a cheerful mix of Asian and European motifs in a free flowing style. The Tree of Life was a favourite theme, intertwined with flowers, animals and birds.

### Defiant dahlias

When most flowers have long since wilted, dahlias still light up the garden with their strong burst of colour. This small-flowered, red dahlia will soldier on until the first frost arrives. The flower owes its name to Andreas Dahlia, an 18th century botanist from Sweden.

### An unruly spirit

This 17th century four-poster bed is from a room at the hotel Le Manoir aux Quat' Saisons, the former Great Milton Manor.

Legend has it that one lord of the manor took to haunting his old bedroom in protest against his widow selling the house. Only when a vicar was called in to exorcise the unruly spirit did peace return. This was in the year of our Lord 1984, no less.

## Patterns all around

As well as looking attractive, the cones in the wooden tray and the pieces of sawn wood (right) are filled with shape and texture. Similarly, the bodice of this brown 19th century gown (left) with its fine bone buttons and crisp pin-tucks can be seen as a strict, very modern motif of lines and dots. In fact, almost everywhere you look, in nature as well as in manufactured objects, there is always fresh inspiration to be had.

## It's all in the looking

As a designer, there is much to be gained from looking at familiar objects in a totally new light. Focusing on form alone, for instance, these old garden tools on the left, hanging neatly side by side in the shed, form an interesting pattern of vertical lines. Likewise, the ceiling (right) with its baskets and sticks makes an intricate motif of lines and dots.

Based on these lines and dots, the 'furesty' cushion (far right) in natural materials is the result of this slightly unorthodox way of observation.

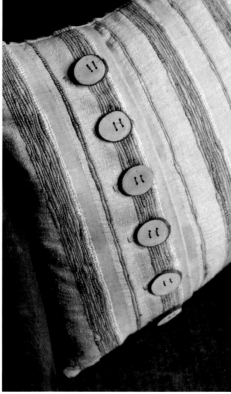

### Wood on display

The sight of freshly chopped logs led me to examine tree ring patterns in more detail. I cut some thin slabs of wood from the branches of various trees for comparison. It turned out that evergreens have particularly interesting cores, especially yews with their nut-like patterned rings.

The resulting slabs of wood were too attractive to hide away so I arranged the most eye-catching in a three-panelled frame. From left to right: yew, box and hazelnut.

### Rustic cushion with beech buttons

For this coarsely textured cushion (above) I chose slabs of beech for buttons and crossed my fingers that the cushion would never have to be washed. The holes in the buttons can be drilled with a hand drill using well dried wood to prevent cracks.

Larger slabs can be used as coasters or placed under vases. By giving them a coat of varnish, you extend their life considerably.

### The kissing gate

The 'kissing gate' (far left) has more to do with cows than canoodling as it prevents livestock from straying. To pass through, the gate touches – or kisses – both sides of the curve.

### Guarding the trees

Forming beautiful patterns, these spiral tree guards have been here for almost a century and protect the bark against horses and deer. Their big iron feet extend deep into the soil ensuring they stay put for many more years to come.

### A parlour for privacy

The drawing room (right) in the south wing of Chalgrove Manor dates from 1505. It is believed to have been the lord of the manor's private quarters or his parlour, which derives from the French *parler*, to talk. The fireplace is from 1680, as is the rich wood panelling. What at first glance looks like intricate wood grain on the panelling is, in fact, a lovely example of 17th century *trompe l'oeil* – the 'grain' has been painted on with a feather.

### The Manor at Chalgrove

Tucked away from the main road lies Chalgrove Manor. A splendid building from the 1400s, its roots go back even further. The Doomsday Book from 1086 notes that Chalgrove's land amounts to 10 hides (around 1,200 acres), enough for twelve ploughs, nine serfs and twenty-three villagers. All valued at the princely sum of £12.

Chalgrove Manor was built over half a century, with the north wing on the right dating back to 1460. The mid-section is from around 1490, and originally consisted of a very high-ceilinged hall. This was the heart of the manor where the household lived and slept and where manorial courts were held. As living conditions became more sophisticated, a first floor was added around 1550, dividing the hall horizontally and thereby creating two new bed chambers. About the same time, a large inglenook fireplace was built into the south wall on the ground floor. The current owners discovered the original fireplace behind six layers of subsequent modifications.

The south wing was added in 1503-05 and appears today more or less as it did 500 years ago. In the old stables, the horses have been replaced by Michael Jacques' busy forge which produces hand-forged metal work of the finest quality.

*Wood, stone and permanence*

### Aromatic coffee balls

The aroma of freshly brewed coffee is irresistible to most people – even if they aren't compulsive coffee drinkers like me. With these coffee balls (left), wafts of fresh coffee will linger on for weeks. Using small, smooth coffee beans with a shiny surface I began by giving some polystyrene balls a coat of brown paint. When dry, I marked the top and bottom. Then, armed with glue, a brush and a cup of coffee, I glued on rows and rows of small shiny beans.

### Rustic textures

The fruits of the season nestle in front of the fireplace. A basket with cedar and pine cones, another with gangly runner beans, a few coffee balls on a piece of firewood; autumn has descended.

### Warm wood tones

Most British seem to prefer polish to paint. Observe their dark wood furniture: how well it suits an autumn day. The rich, wooden surfaces positively ooze warmth, tranquillity and a sense of permanence.

# Wistful beauty

### Potpourri or a rotten pot

Potpourri has been made since medieval times, but rather than drying the flowers, aromatic petals and spices were usually preserved in a saline solution. The sodden concoction didn't look particularly attractive so it was kept in a pot with a latticed lid to allow the scent to permeate. Potpourri literally means *rotten pot* in French.

### The last flowers of summer

Dried roses, peonies and hydrangea make a wistful reminder of distant summer days.

### Dried roses in the cowshed

The old cowshed has hardly changed since the inter-war years when it was last in use. The posts that used to keep the cow's head locked during milking still remain in place (far left of room). The shed is cool and dry with only a modicum of light which makes it an ideal place for drying flowers. Bunches of roses hang here to dry for a couple of weeks at a time and petals are prepared for sweet smelling potpourri.

### Fortepiano as a fashion accessory

This mahogany-cased square piano, or fortepiano, was built in London in 1780 by a Christopher Ganer who began his career building harpsichords. Responding to the growing demand for more powerful instruments, he specialised in fortepianos with improved mechanics and a larger tone to enable the sound to fill the new, larger concert halls. Fortepianos rapidly became coveted fashion items.

### An English violin

This violin is my old and trusted friend, made by one Matthew Furber of London in 1800. At that time, violins had shorter necks and strings were less tightly strung, yielding a smaller tone than we are used to today. The majority of old violins, mine too, have been modified to produce a fuller sound.

### Roses on the panelling

Candles from the two brass wall sconces add a soft glow to the fine 17th century panelling. Bunches of dried roses frame a Dutch painting from the same century.

### A brace of pheasants

Geoff Oliver (left), shooting instructor and gamekeeper, returns with a brace of pheasants. The birds are then hung outside for a few days before they are plucked or skinned – according to time and temperament.

### Asian guests

The Common Pheasant looks anything but common in the countryside. Not surprising really, since it is of Asian origin. The Romans are said to have introduced the breed to Britain nearly two thousand years ago.

### Strutting dandies

The pheasant cock is a vain fellow. In spring, he struts about, flaunting his fine feathers while crowing loudly with a peculiarly resonant sound, so unlike other birds. He attracts a whole harem of hens – the more the merrier – and mates them all. Each hen lays around a dozen eggs which hatch in just over three weeks. The chicks grow quickly and reach adult size in less than four months.

The Common Pheasant cock is not the only spectacular pheasant in Britain. Golden and Silver Pheasants have vibrant colours too, and the orange tipped feathers of Lady Amherst are equally splendid.

### A meal fit for a king

The pheasant shares its genes with the peacock, which is arguably the most magnificent of the two. Peacocks were introduced to Britain in medieval times and both types of birds were considered delicacies at the royal table. Roasted peacock, served whole with a gilded beak and arranged in its magnificent plumage, is listed among the dishes at the court of Henry VIII. Reassuringly, the bird *was* plucked before being roasted.

## Pheasant stationery

Designing your own cards is
easy if you have a computer
and a graphics programme.
For these cards, I scanned in a
variety of feathers and adjusted
their lengths to create a series
of more equally sized motifs. I
created a misty effect by
reducing opacity to 40% and
chose a creamy colour as
background. The finished
images were printed on to
glazed paper and glued on
to good quality white card.
For the penholder, I printed
one long panel of feathers.

## Cushion with pheasant feathers

Feathers are beautiful, but not particularly practical in soft interiors as they do not wash well. An easy and fun idea is this feather cushion. The feathers have been pushed through the suede and are kept in place by double-sided tape. The fine orange-tipped feathers come from a diamond pheasant, or Lady Amherst, the others are from a Common Pheasant. Needless to say, this is not a robust design so don't use expensive materials. This particular suede cushion cost £2 at a market stall.

## Stationery box from a bygone age

Handwritten letters have become something of a rarity, which is a shame since so much of the sender's personality is reflected in his or her particular hand. The abundance of old stationery boxes is a reminder of just how essential letter writing used to be. This walnut box is English and dates from the 19th century. Stationery boxes differ widely; some have only a few slots for paper and envelopes, others are almost fully portable offices complete with inkwells, writing tablet, perpetual calendar and numerous drawers.

### A sprig of red leaves
For this November table, I went for warm, rich colours. Tied on with string, a sprig of red leaves and hip berries decorate the back of each chair. If place cards are required, why not hang them here for a change?

### Autumnal table setting
A dash of colour sets off the whiteness of the tablemats and napkins to good effect. Next to each plate, I placed an orange Chinese lantern and a Cape gooseberry. They are botanical 'cousins' of the *Physalis* family.

## Pheasant pie
*serves 8*

'You *never* cook pheasant?' My father was decidedly unimpressed with his student daughter's lack of gastronomic diversity (and budget). I hope this makes up for it:

*900 g pheasant, boned*  
*2 tbsp butter*  
*2 tbsp olive oil*  
*2 onions, chopped*  
*3 cloves garlic, crushed*  
*150 g mushrooms, sliced*  

*150 g streaky bacon*  
*2 tbsp plain flour*  
*1 orange, juice and zest*  
*1 bay leaf*  
*550 ml stock*  
*550 ml red wine*  

*1 tbsp redcurrant jelly*  
*salt and pepper*  
*400 g shortcrust pastry*  
*1 beaten egg*  

Brown the meat in half the butter and oil. Put aside. Fry the onions in the rest of the butter and oil until soft. Add garlic, mushrooms and bacon. Cook for 5 mins. Add the flour and cook for a further 2–3 mins. Add orange zest and juice, bay leaf, stock, wine and jelly. Add the meat and season. Simmer for 40–50 mins. Place the mixture in an ovenproof dish. Cover with a lid of shortcrust pastry. Cut a hole in the lid (for steam). Decorate with pastry feathers, brush with egg and bake at 200° C until golden (about 20 mins). Serve with redcurrant jelly.

## Vibrant fruit
The vibrant colours of the fruit render any flower arrangement superfluous. Rows of cherries and Cape gooseberries make eye-catching appetizers and taste delicious served with freshly baked bread and a glass of red wine.

## Ornamental pumpkins

Some ornamental pumpkins, or gourds, are edible but most are grown for their eye-catching colours and texture. Dried, they gain a softer, more poetic beauty.

## Pumpkins on the compost

This compost is working 'double shift'. The middle section is gradually filled with the year's harvest of garden waste, which will compost for at least six months. The other sections have finished 'brewing' and now provide a fertile bed for the edible pumpkins until the compost is required.

### Pumpkin soufflé          serves 8

| | | |
|---|---|---|
| 300 ml pumpkin flesh* | 1½ tsp cinnamon | ¼ tsp salt and pepper |
| 180 g sugar | 1½ tsp ground ginger | 500 ml milk |
| 6 tbsp butter | ½ tsp nutmeg | 9 eggs, separated |
| 180 g plain flour | ¼ tsp ground cloves | Icing sugar for dusting |

*Pumpkin purée: either buy a can of 150 ml pumpkin purée or make your own in which case peel the 300 ml pumpkins, remove seeds, dice and bake at 220° C for 25 mins until soft. Add sugar. Measure out 150 ml for the soufflé.

Soufflé: grease 8 ovenproof ramekins. Heat the butter in a small saucepan and add flour, spices and seasoning. Cook for 2–3 mins, stirring continuously to prevent browning. Gradually add the milk. Remove the saucepan from the heat and stir well to avoid lumps. Return the pan to the heat and slowly bring to the boil, stirring constantly. Boil for 1–2 mins, still stirring. Remove the saucepan from the heat again, add the pumpkin purée and egg yolks and mix well. Whisk the egg whites until stiff and carefully fold them into the mixture. Spoon into the ramekins and bake at 175° C for 30–35 mins until the soufflés have risen well over the rim of the ramekins. Dust with icing sugar and serve immediately.

*Quiet, unassuming beauty*

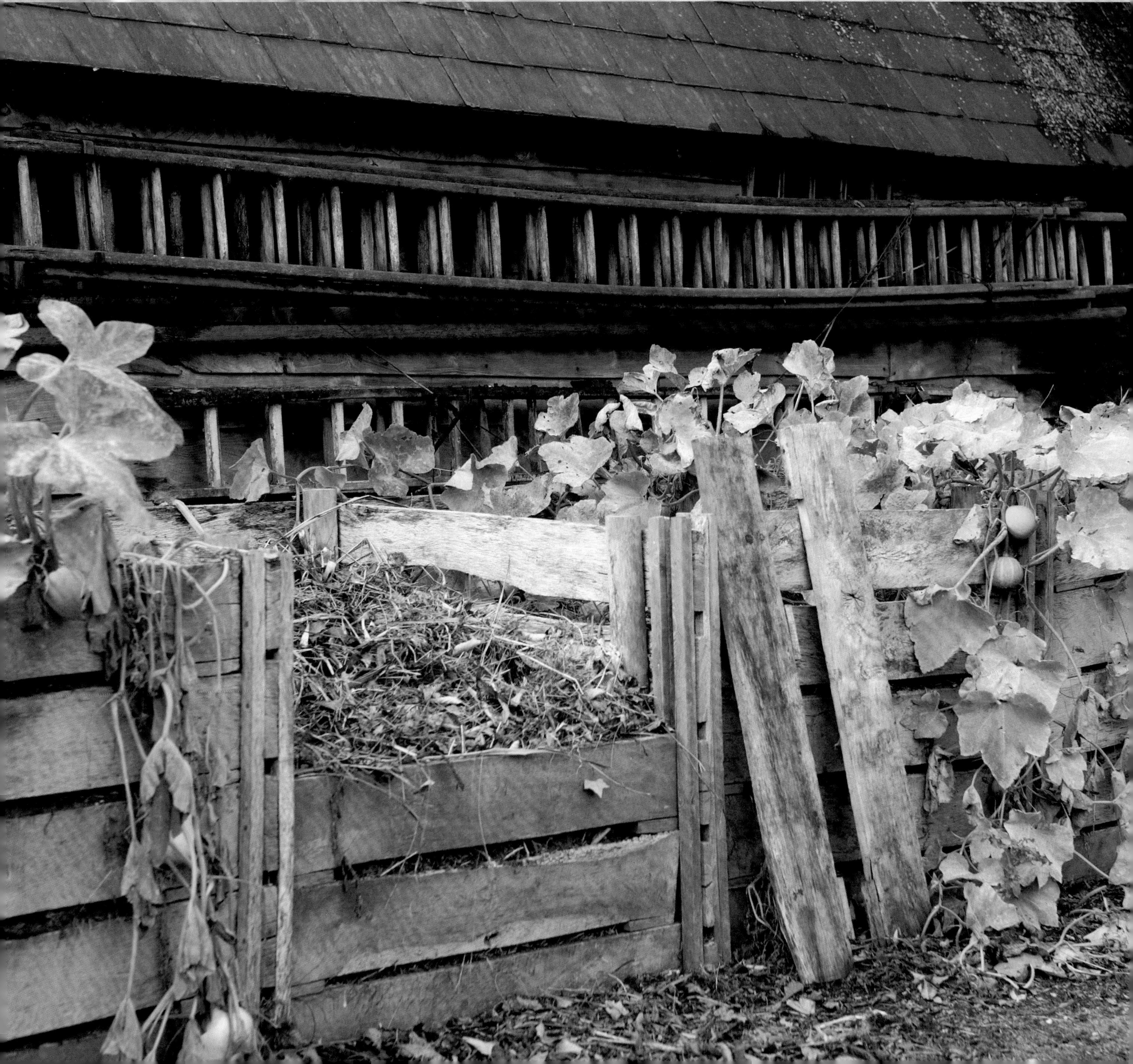

### Chinese lanterns

The Chinese lantern (left) is so decorative. If cut, it retains its shape and colour for years. If left to wither in the garden, the lantern will transform into the finest gossamer bauble.

### Jack-o'-lanterns

Irish settlers brought the Halloween custom of Jack-o'-lanterns to America, replacing their customary turnips with pumpkins. Here, pretty geometrical patterns replace the customary scary masks.

### Halloween and Hallowmass

The Celts started it all with their Day of the Dead on November 1. The festival was then adapted into All Hallows Day by the Christian church. Also known as All Saints Day, it became the day to honour Christian saints. Celebrations on All Hallows Eve, or Halloween, revolved around death and the occult, a custom still maintained today when children (and the occasional adult) dress up in ghoulish outfits and play trick-or-treat or the traditional apple bobbin. All Souls Day on November 2 completes the three days of *Hallowmass*.

### Light on a dark night

The scarlet crab apples add a sparkle to the last glimmer of daylight. It is time to light the candles and celebrate Halloween.

These leaf lanterns are made from drinking glasses and screw top jars. Stick on a row or two of fresh leaves in bright colours with double-sided tape. Tie some string or sisal around them. If the lantern needs a handle, use screw top jars and wind thin wire around the grooves at the top.

**Toffee apples**  *serves 7*

*7 wooden skewers  250 ml water*

*7 dessert apples   175 g golden syrup*

*400 g granulated sugar*

Remove the stalks and fix the apples securely on to a wooden skewer. Pour sugar, water and syrup into a thick-bottomed saucepan. Heat while stirring continuously until the sugar has dissolved. Bring to the boil and allow to simmer without stirring until the temperature has reached 150° C. Dip the apples in the toffee and cover evenly. Place on greaseproof paper brushed with oil. Allow to set. Serve with a fruity drink.

**Bonfire night**

36 barrels of gun powder, 13 Catholics and 1 Protestant king. The year is 1605, the time of the infamous Gunpowder Plot. On November 5, a group of aggrieved Roman Catholics attempted to blow up king and parliament. One of the conspirators, Guy Fawkes, was caught red-handed, the plot was foiled and Fawkes was hung, drawn and quartered. To celebrate the safe deliverance of James I, bonfires were lit all over England, and in 1606, a law was passed making the celebration of November 5 compulsory – just to be on the safe side. The law remained in force for 250 years.

# The spirit of winter

A blanket of heavy mist covers the landscape and for a fleeting moment the world
is entirely your own. The garden lies dormant, but has left small patches of
greenery here and there. The cedar tree stands tall, shedding its mighty cones
as it has done for so many generations.

# Winter

When icicles hang by the wall,

And Dick the shepherd blows his nail,

And Tom bears logs into the hall,

And milk comes frozen home in pail,

When blood is nipp'd and ways be foul,

Then nightly sings the staring owl -

To-who;

Tu-whit, Tu-who, a merry note,

While greasy Joan doth keel the pot.

William Shakespeare

(1564–1616)

### Frozen stars

In the early morning frost, the *Phlomis italica* looks like nature's own Christmas decorations. In summer, small pink flowers shoot up between its woolly leaves, but now it looks for all the world like a frozen star.

### Ice hearts on trees

Frost and snow in Oxfordshire is a rare but beautiful sight. Children can't wait to get outside. Here, then, is a suggestion for some real ice art. They will need water, thin wire and ice-trays with heart-shapes, stars, or the like. Larger moulds are preferable for the ice art to be visible from a distance. Fill the moulds with water and perhaps a few drops of water colour or food dye. For handles, cut 25 cm pieces of wire, bend them in half and immerse the ends in the water. Freeze and hang the ice hearts on a branch outside a window.

### Frosted fruit

*various fruits*
*1–2 large egg whites*
*castor sugar*

Beat the egg whites lightly
with a fork and brush over
the fruit. To prepare the sugar
coating, hold the larger fruits
by their stalks and fix smaller
fruits on to a skewer. Dust
thoroughly with sugar. Leave
to dry on sugar covered
greaseproof paper or let
them dry on the skewers.
Do not touch as finger marks
will show. Enjoy as a sweet or
as a decoration.

Winter   161

## Maple leaf calendar

The sight of bright red maple leaves on bare branches (right) was the inspiration behind this unorthodox advent calendar with 25 pouches of goodies (left). To make it, draw a leaf pattern with a straight top for the opening. Fold over a non-fraying fabric, e.g. synthetic velvet, and cut out 25 double leaves. Machine zigzag each leaf together leaving the top open. Hand sew two rows of silver running thread along the top to make a draw-string handle. Write the date on each bag with a textile pen.

### The Japanese maple

The garden is clad in the muted colours of winter. Suddenly, there is a burst of scarlet from the few remaining maple leaves. What a marvellous sight! Store it in your library of ideas to use for future designs.

### Advent wreath with crystals

Frosty lavender inspired this advent wreath (right). I placed a ready-made crystal wreath on a silver dish and popped 4 silver candles into small candlesticks. Silver baubles and real poinsettia leaves completed the effect.

### Spicy Christmas decorations

If you are short of materials for Christmas decorations, a rummage in the kitchen cupboard might help. Dried slices of oranges, small chillis, cinnamon sticks, cloves and nuts add scent and character.

### Peace in the forest

The early morning frost has disappeared and the forest releases a soft smell of soil and pine. Maybe you'll come across some holly, some ivy and a cone or two. Perhaps there is even a touch of snow in the air. This, to me, truly heralds the arrival of Christmas.

The forest has long since finished its Christmas preparations. The Christmas trees were selected in late summer, and in October the great felling operation began. Come December, all is quiet in the forest again.

### Majestic cones

Cones from the cedar tree are immense. With their peculiarly dense structure, they look stunning on a mantelpiece or on the Christmas table, particularly if they are given a light touch of gold or silver spray.

### Pearl droplets

The raindrops cling to the twigs like pearls on a string. Make your own raindrops by decorating fresh sprigs with pearls. Give the twigs a light layer of gold spray. Thread pearls on to golden string and secure with a small bead at the bottom. Attach to the sprigs. Finish off with a piece of lace ribbon.

### Harry Lauder's walking stick

If I didn't like it for its shape, I'd love it for its names. 'Contorted Filbert', 'Harry Lauder's walking stick' and 'Corylus avellana Contorta' are all names for Corkscrew Hazel.

### Nature's decorations

Acorns and corkscrew hazel look lovely with a little gold and glitter. But don't be too heavy-handed – spray lightly, allowing the under-lying colour and structure to show through.

### Golden gifts

The presents are wrapped in fabric and tissue paper in a palette of green and gold. Use remnants of plush fabric or stitch together a silk bag and decorate with honesty, ivy and dried roses.

### Stoic tulips

Red tulips peep out from their fir-covered winter bed. When cut, the tulips will only last a day, but these Tulipa Brilliant Star are uncut, and their bulbs are still in place. Nestling in the fir, they will last for weeks as long as it is neither too warm nor too cold.

### Festooned with holly

For the garland (right), cut bunches of 25 cm long fir sprigs. Take a long rope, hold one bunch against it at a time and secure with green wire. Continue until the entire rope is covered. Add holly and lights.

### Gingerbread hearts

There never seems to be a shortage of helpers when we bake ginger-bread biscuits. Try and save a few for Christmas tree decorations as they look great and will last for years.

The dough:

*375 g plain flour*

*1 egg, beaten*

*1 tsp cinnamon & 2 tsp ground ginger*

*½ tsp bicarbonate of soda*

*120 g butter*

*4 tbsp golden syrup*

*175 g muscovado sugar*

Sift the flour into a bowl, add the egg, spices and bicarbonate of soda. Rub in the butter to make a breadcrumb-like texture. Heat the syrup in a saucepan and add to the mixture. Add the sugar. Mix to a soft dough and knead until smooth. Roll out to a thickness of 3–4 mm. Cut into shapes using a pastry cutter. Make holes for ribbons. Bake for 8–10 mins at 190° C.

Royal icing:

*1 egg white*

*250 g icing sugar*

*¼ tbsp lemon juice*

Whisk the egg white with a fork. Stir in the icing sugar. Add lemon juice and mix until the icing is smooth and keeps its shape. Use an icing bag with a small nozzle (plain, no.3) to decorate the cold biscuits. Thread a silk ribbon through the hole.

## Angel cards and hearts

Making your own Christmas cards is not as time consuming as you may think, particularly if you make a whole series in one go. For these cards, I used the seed cases of the honesty plant for the angels' wings. I also needed a silver pen, remnants of fabric, lace and paper of various textures.

The hearts (below) are of the same design and colour as the cards. The 'wings' are made from tulle and silver thread. Fill the hearts with cloves, lavender or other herbs and spices.

## Christmas cards

The first Christmas cards arrive and are ceremoniously arranged on the mantelpiece. Then panic ensues as dozens of cards still remain to be written. However laborious, exchanging Christmas greetings is a tradition most people wouldn't be without. It dates back to 1843 when Sir Henry Cole commissioned the first Christmas card. With drastic reductions in postage rates, the practice of sending Christmas cards soon took off. In the 1860s, it spread to America where the German Louis Prang cornered the market.

## Visit from Father Christmas

On Christmas Eve, churches open their doors for the celebratory midnight mass, Christ's Mass, which gave Christmas its name.

A mince pie and sherry await Father Christmas when he comes down the chimney laden with presents. King Winter, his pagan forebear, was far less jolly, handing out both punishments as well as rewards. The American Santa Claus derives from the Dutch Sinter Klaas.

*The silent beauty of rain*

### Majestic pampas grass

The sun has just dried the last raindrops and the huge plumes of the pampas grass wave in the wind. Exotic and grandiose, pampas grass looks as if it ought to grow somewhere much warmer. Indeed, this was the case prior to the 1840s when it was introduced to Europe from its native South Africa. Nowadays, it is surprisingly common on these shores, which shows that the pampas, or *Cortaderia selloana*, can easily thrive in the British climate.

### Soft rain drops

Apparently, the Eskimos have more than forty words to describe different types of snow. Perhaps we should have the same number of words for rain. My favourite rain is that soft and gentle kind which caresses you as it falls, making the soil smell all fertile and fresh.

### Pearls of rain

Droplets of rain, frozen in time, have been brought indoors. These glass beads (right) will look attractive on the Christmas tree or, as here, on a branch of corkscrew hazel. As the branch is light, it can easily be hung from a near invisible fishing line.

### Christmas wrapping

The presents on the top of the cupboard (left) are wrapped in remnants of fine wallpaper. The thickness of the paper adds a touch of luxury, as do the lace ribbons and handmade paper streamers cut with pinking shears.

### Proud angels

The angels (right) are dried poppy seed heads on stems which are painted white. The dresses are made from dried hydrangeas fixed with thin thread and lots of patience! Spray white and add silver glitter.

### A ring of roses

This wreath requires you to ruthlessly cut the stems of 35 roses to a mere 5 cm. Line a basket with plastic and fill with wet oasis. Arrange two rows of roses. To fix each candle in place, use four cocktail sticks secured with floral tape. Add crystals & glitter.

### Gustavian Christmas

The vintage dress (right) was the starting point for my choice of colours in this Christmas setting. The colour palette comprises cream, pink, silvery blue and soft green.

The two floral patterned Swedish armchairs are from the 18th century, as is the portrait. The Gustavian-style white chairs and mirror date from the 19th century. A garland of ivy hangs from the fireplace and on the mirror is a fir wreath decorated with silver cones and beauty berries.

### Christmas Cossacks

Christmas isn't Christmas without crackers. *Cosaques*, as they were originally called, were invented in 1846 by Tom Smith, a clever confectioner from London who was looking to improve sales. First he tried wrapping his sweets in coloured paper. Sales rose slightly. Then he added a novelty to each parcel. Sales improved a little more. Finally, he hit upon the idea of adding strips of saltpetre to the goodies to create a bang. Tom Smith was in business.

### The Puritans didn't approve

Christmas is a time of joy when everyone is free to celebrate as they wish. This was not always the case. Almost four hundred years ago, Oliver Cromwell and his Puritan government forbade all festivities and decorations and Christmas Day was declared an ordinary working day. Soldiers patrolled the streets to reinforce the clampdown and anyone who was caught celebrating risked arrest. Across the Atlantic, Puritans in Boston introduced a similar ban, that lasted for twenty-two years.

### Mistletoe wreath

The mistletoe wreath to the right is supported on a sturdy wire wreath form. Secure the sprigs of mistletoe with green wire. Add a little glitter glue in silver and blue and tie a lace bow on top. The leaves will keep fresh for a surprisingly long time, but the poisonous berries soon drop off.

## A glimpse of heaven

The Christmas tree was made popular in England by Prince Albert who introduced this German tradition into Victorian England in the 1840s. There are many theories as to how the decorated tree originated. My favourite relates to Martin Luther (1483-1546) who, when walking through the forest one cold winter's night, was struck by the sight of shimmering stars between the tree tops. On his return home, he is said to have decorated a tree with candles to give his children 'a glimpse of heaven'.

## All that glitters

Shiny baubles and other manufactured Christmas decorations became increasingly popular in Britain from the 1870s. Prior to that, trees were decorated with sweets and handmade coloured paper decorations, a tradition that still thrives in my native Scandinavia where it is not uncommon to hang a few pieces of homemade 'art' filled with sweets among the baubles.

## White Christmas decorations

For the *snow crystal* (right): use pine twigs, a small polystyrene ball, feathers, pva glue, beads, thin wire, glitter and paint. Paint ball and twigs white. Glue beads on to the twigs. Push twigs and feathers into the ball. Thread beads on a wire and wind around the ball. The *cornet* (far right) is made using stiff card, white paper, white velvet, silk ribbon, dried rosebuds, spray glue and pva glue. Make a cornet out of stiff card, cover with velvet and spray glue on. Glue a silk ribbon handle on to the inside. Make a slightly smaller inner cone from the paper. Insert into the cornet. Place a row of dried rosebuds between the inner and outer cones and glue roses and cone in place. Add a silk ribbon to the rim of the cornet.

## Clam soup for New Year

*serves 5*

| | |
|---|---|
| *3 kg raw clam shells* | *4 tbsp butter* |
| *150 ml shellfish stock (see method)* | *125 g cream cheese* |
| *150 ml vegetable stock* | *200 ml double cream* |
| *4 shallots, chopped* | *salt and pepper* |
| *2 cloves garlic, crushed* | *100 ml grated cheese* |
| *1 red pepper, chopped* | *chives, chopped* |

Clean and rinse the clam shells in cold water. All live clams will close when rinsed; discard any that remain open. Put the live clams in an empty saucepan and steam until they open again. Take up the clams and check they have all opened; if not, discard. Measure 150 ml shellfish stock and mix with the vegetable stock. Set aside. Remove about 2/3 of the cooked clams from their shells and keep a third in their shells to decorate when serving. Gently fry the onions, garlic and red pepper in butter and allow to simmer for a couple of minutes. Add the cream cheese, stock, cream, salt and pepper. Add all the clams. Pour into an ovenproof dish and cover with grated cheese. Bake at 200° C for 5 mins. Serve in portions, sprinkle with chopped chives.

### New Year's table in the winter garden

The peacock fountain (far left) was the *leit-motif* for this New Year's lunch decoration. I put some wet oasis on a tray and covered it with fern. An up-turned candlestick served as a fountain and was secured with wire. Filled with blue marbles, the base of the candlestick became a fine 'water basin'. I placed a small peacock on the rim and topped it all off with shiny baubles.

### Framed bottles

This spare window (left) has become a multi-frame for bottle motifs. To make the images, I decided to use a scanner instead of a camera because I like the interesting side-effects of blurred colours and shadows which result from scanning in low resolution ('draft' quality setting). I printed out the images on glossy paper, cut each image to size and glued it behind the pane.

### Medicine bottles from the garden

Now and then, we come across an old glass bottle in the garden discarded perhaps by a farm hand a hundred or so years ago. The bottles often contained medicine, mainly for horses, or a household product. Highly decorative and popular collectors' items, the coloured bottles look very attractive on a window sill or as miniature vases.

### Magic in twilight

The sight of the potting shed window in the twilight (right), with its silhouetted tools and bottles, holds a peculiarly poetic beauty. It was this that sparked the idea for the silhouetted bottles in the frame.

### Heaven scent

In the chill of winter, the greenhouse is a veritable haven of warmth and scent. The perfume from hyacinths, early narcissus and winter geraniums gives a real lift to the senses. Try rubbing a geranium leaf with your fingers and you are rewarded with the spicy aroma of lemon and mint.

This greenhouse is divided into two areas: one is kept warmish at 15–16° C throughout the winter while the other is colder, but never below 7° C. The mousetraps testify to the popularity of this snug winter retreat.

### Winter watering

Watering a greenhouse this size is no mean feat. Under the plant tables, the old zinc watering cans are lined up next to ferns and other plants that do not need much light.

### White hyacinths

Forcing hyacinths during
the autumn has paid off.
After unfolding slowly for
a few weeks in the green-
house, the blooms now
stand tall and splendid and
give off a glorious scent.

At Christmas time,
hyacinths often form part
of larger arrangements, but
January calls for simplicity.
Plant them in individual
clay pots, or put them in
those special glass bulb
vases designed for one
hyacinth and its bulb.

*The dovecote is still here*

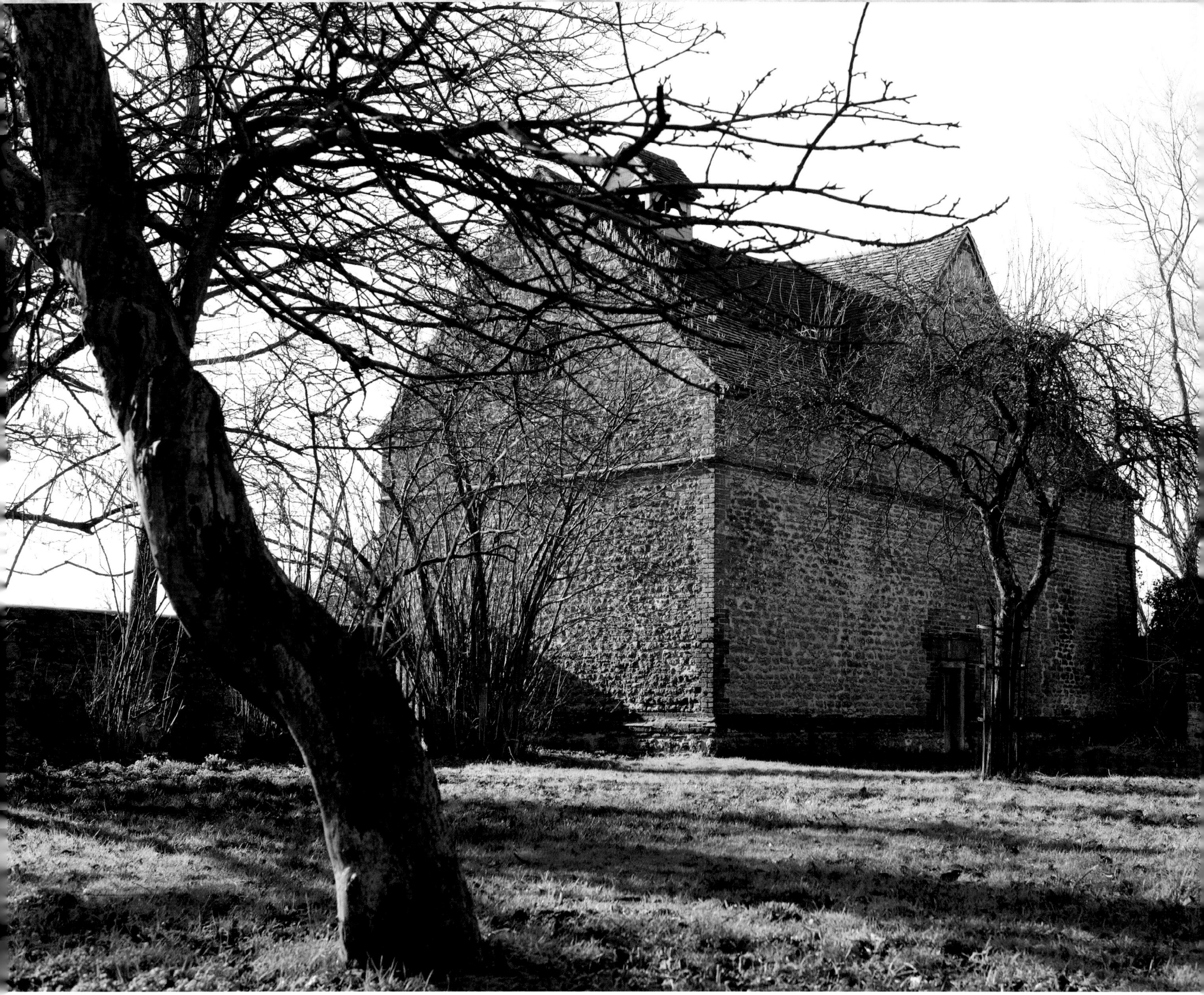

### The dovecote at Culham Manor

This sturdy stone building (left) is a dovecote from 1685. At that time, keeping pigeons was the preserve of the landed gentry as only large households could afford such extravagant luxury. Owning a dovecote was highly prestigious and until the 1600s, it was a privilege granted to manor houses and protected by law.

### Young delicacies

The design of a dovecote was dictated by the fashion of the time, but the purpose remained the same: rearing squabs, or unfledged pigeons. This was not because households ran short of fresh meat in winter. Early household accounts show that large estates were fully capable of procuring fresh produce all year round, but a delicacy like squabs required special care. In the wild, squabs are fed for the first four weeks after which they are thrown out of the nest and left to fend for themselves. By breeding them in captivity, the young pigeons could be taken just before they were ready to fly, with their flying muscles still undeveloped. This resulted in the coveted tender meat. Adult, muscular pigeons were utterly undesirable and only given to servants.

### Not quite empty

It is dark and still and you feel very insignificant inside this colossal dovecote. The only source of light is high up under the cupola where the pigeons fly in and out. The nesting holes, 3,000 in all, extend from floor to ceiling on each wall. A solitary pigeon watches the intruder from its vantage point high above the ground. The owner's initials from 1685 remain above the door and you get an uneasy feeling he is still around.

### Fairmaids of February

Every year, I get the same feeling of joy when I spot the first common snowdrop, the *Galanthus nivalis* (above). The *Galanthus plicatus* is another well-known 'white lady', which was introduced into England in the 1850s by British soldiers who brought it back from the trenches in war-torn Crimea. The snowdrops in the vases (left) are the tall *Galanthus S. Arnott*, which grow to an impressive 25 cm in height. To prevent them from overturning, I made a grid of sellotape across the rim of the vases and stuck the stems through the holes.

### The monks at Culham Manor

Across from the church lies Culham Manor, as it has done since the 15th century. Owned by the Abbey of Abingdon, it was originally built to house elderly clerics. Here, the monks saw out their final years in pleasant surroundings. They constructed a fine fish pond (facing page, bottom) overseen by a solitary monk. He continues to spew out water to this day.

### A house with a history

The idyll came to an abrupt end in Culham when, in 1538, Henry VIII turned against the Catholic Church. The manor was confiscated and sold to William Bury, a wool trader from London, for the price of £600 plus some of his land in Kent. This was a handsome sum, even for a King, but then the house was close to the Thames and the town of Abingdon, England's oldest market town. Bury's descendants lie in the churchyard opposite the manor. The house has been altered and extended over the years, but many fine details have been preserved. The wonderful wide oak doors and the Flemish stained glass windows all help to form a patchwork of history.

### As beautiful as a Flemish painting

A huge plaited bread awaits the guests in this 17th century dining room.

*Serves 20*

| | |
|---|---|
| *2 tbsp dried yeast* | *2 tsp salt* |
| *1 tsp sugar (for yeast)* | *1 tbsp sugar (for dough)* |
| *900 ml lukewarm water* | *90 g butter* |
| *1.5 kg plain flour* | *1 egg for glazing* |

Whisk the dried yeast with 100 ml of the water and one 1 tsp sugar. Allow to stand for 10–15 mins until frothy. Mix the flour, salt and 1 tbsp sugar and add the butter. Add the yeast mixture together with the rest of the lukewarm water. Knead the dough on a floured surface until it becomes soft and elastic but not sticky. Return the dough to the bowl and cover with cling film brushed with a little oil. Leave to rise for about 1½ hours to double in size. Beat the dough and divide it into three portions. Roll each portion into approx. 50 cm long sections. Plait the three lengths and shape into one large ring. Cover with a tea towel and leave to rise in a warm place to double in size. Brush with egg and bake at 190° C for 40–45 mins until golden brown. Cool on a wire tray.

## Root vegetable soup

*serves 8*

*50 g butter*

*2 tbsp olive oil*

*4 carrots*

*2 medium potatoes*

*2 sweet potatoes*

*2 turnips*

*2 large onions*

*1 small swede*

*2 tsp freshly grated ginger*

*475 ml stock (veg or meat)*

*salt and pepper*

*475 ml milk*

*150 ml crème fraîche*

*2 tbsp fresh dill, chopped*

*dill sprigs to garnish*

Melt the butter and olive oil in a large saucepan. Chop the vegetables and grate the ginger. Add to the saucepan and gently fry for 10 mins, stirring occasionally. Add the stock, bring to the boil and season. Cover and simmer for 25–30 mins until the vegetables are cooked.

Remove the soup from the heat and put in the blender. Return the puréed vegetables to the pan, add the milk and slowly reheat. Take the soup off the heat again, add the crème fraîche and chopped dill. Serve in soup bowls and garnish with sprigs of dill.

## Winter warmers

The irresistible smell of piping hot cottage pie wafts through this cottage kitchen. Thanks to the British, who introduced me to this dish, it is now a favourite in our kitchen. Root vegetable soup is another hearty dish for winter. It is as scrumptious as it is filling.

## Cottage pie
*serves 8–10*

**Meat sauce:**

| | | |
|---|---|---|
| 2 tbsp olive oil | 475 ml stock | |
| 2 onions, chopped | 1 tbsp Worcestershire sauce | |
| 2 carrots, sliced | 2 tbsp tomato ketchup | |
| 2 celery sticks | 2 tbsp tomato paste | |
| 1.5 kg minced beef | 2 bay leaves | |
| 1 tbsp plain flour | salt and black pepper | |

**Topping:**

1.25 kg potatoes, diced
100 ml whole milk
100 ml cream
50 g butter
salt
white pepper

Meat sauce: gently fry onions, carrots and celery sticks in oil for a few mins. Add meat and cook for about 10 mins. Add flour and cook a further 2 mins. Add stock and the rest of ingredients. Season with salt and black pepper and simmer for 30–40 mins. Leave to cool.

Topping: boil the diced potatoes until soft, then mash. Add the milk, cream and butter. Mix to a light consistency and add salt and white pepper to taste. Pour the meat sauce into a greased ovenproof dish and spoon the mashed potatoes evenly on top. Use a fork to make a pattern and place the dish in a hot oven at 190° C for 30–35 mins until golden brown.

### Latticework in the garden

Intricate iron gates add charm and character to any garden. Wrought iron became hugely popular in England at the end of the 17th century. At that time, France led the way in the manufacture of beautiful gates and latticework and French artisans were eventually enticed to come to England to teach local blacksmiths their craft. Many of the gates and ornate features we admire today were made locally in the 18th century in what became known as the 'English style', even though it was originally French.

### Patterns from nature

The echo of hammering fills the air and metal parts are scattered all around the workshop. From garden gates to church candelabra, master blacksmith Michael Jaques and his team create splendid one-off designs. His is the hand behind the iron gate with the scroll finish (facing page, top right).

The snail plant (left) is an amusing example of how any conceivable pattern already exists in nature.

### Red berries in the garden

Even in the depths of winter, there are still sparks of colour in the garden. The red crab apples are particularly tenacious, lasting into February, as do the delicate pink berries of the common spindle, *Euonymus europeus*. The pink capsules and orange seeds look attractive both fresh and dried. The Spindle tree is so named because its wood was used to make spindles for spinning.

### A mutable martyr

Valentine's Day is regarded by many as an American custom, but like Halloween, Valentine's Day actually originated in Europe, crossed the Atlantic and then returned to Europe in a new guise.

Although several saints share the name Valentine, the saint we commonly associate with love and romance would seem to be the Valentine martyred in 280 AD. In Northern Europe, in the early Middle Ages, he was the patron saint of epilepsy sufferers, but by the late Middle Ages he had metamorphosed into the saint of loving couples. One explanation for this change claims that it was because his feast day, February 14, fell during the mating season of birds.

### A Valentine heart

A red heart is the symbol
of Valentine's Day. This one
is made from the last crab
apples of winter. Thread the
crab apples on to a piece
of strong wire. Make into a
heart shape. Twist the wire
together at the top and
attach a ribbon to hang it
from. As the weight of the
berries can pull the heart
out of shape, I cheated a
little by tying a fishing line
from beneath the bow to
the tip of the heart.

## Cosseted at Le Manoir

Le Manoir aux Quat' Saisons is *the* place to celebrate Valentine's Day. *Patron* Raymond Blanc has transformed the former Great Milton Manor into a gastronomic temple in charming surroundings. The 15th century manor provides a tranquil and stylish setting for its guests who are pampered from the moment they arrive. But enter the kitchen and it's a different world: a place of hectic activity where sublime dishes are produced with skill and dedication.

## Chequerboard biscuits

Courtesy of Patissier Benoir Blin,
Le Manoir aux Quat' Saisons.

*20–30 biscuits*

White shortbread:

*50 g icing sugar*

*1 egg yolk (keep egg white for brushing)*

*80 g unsalted butter*

*Pinch of salt*

*120 g plain flour*

Chocolate shortbread:

*50 g icing sugar*

*1 egg yolk (keep egg white for brushing)*

*80 g unsalted butter*

*pinch of salt*

*80 g plain flour*

*40 g cocoa powder*

Method:

Prepare each shortbread dough separately like this. Mix together the icing sugar, egg yolk, softened butter and a pinch of salt in a large bowl. Add flour to the butter mixture (for dark dough, add flour *and* cocoa powder) and rub together with your fingertips to make a 'sandy' texture. Lightly flour the work surface and knead the dough with the palms of your hands until well mixed, a little more vigorously for the last few seconds. Wrap the dough in cling film and refrigerate for about 20 mins.

To form the chequered pattern: roll out each piece of dough into a 15 cm square, about 7-8 mm thick. Keep an even thickness because of the pattern. Using the egg white, stick the dark square on top of the white. Cut into two halves, brush with egg white and place one on top of the other so that you now have an oblong 'sandwich' of white, dark, white, dark.

Cut lengthways into 8 thin strips. Take 4 of these strips, place one on top of the other to produce a chessboard effect. Stick together with egg white. Repeat with the remaining 4 strips. You now have two strips of 4 x 4 chequered light and dark dough ready for slicing. Cut the strips into about 1 cm thick biscuits and place them on greased baking paper. Bake at 180° C for about 10 mins.

### The forgotten medlar tree

If snow is a rarity in the South of England, we do have a fair number of frosty nights, which is just what the once common medlar (left) needs for its fruit to start to ripen. Once picked, the fruit should be put in a cold, dark place to *blet* (literally to 'over ripe'). By the time the fruit is soft, yellow and looks decidedly past it, it's ready.

To make a medlar fool, fold in 100 ml whipped cream and a portion of custard and mix with around 300 ml of sweetened medlar pulp. Don't overmix. Enjoy with a glass of port.

### Intricate bark structures

The trees stand dark against the white background, emphasising the gnarled structure of the old bark. With its infinite patterns, bark is a fascinating motif to work with. One can either focus on its three dimensional qualities or seek out surface patterns such as in birch tree bark where the texture lies in the white and beige markings. Sometimes whole pieces of birch bark peel off from the trunk. Thin and even, they can be used as paper.

## Bark books from the garden

My sketchbook shows experiments with bark texture. I used silk screen printing, but a camera and a computer will do just as well. Take a close-up of a bark texture and transfer to the computer. Use its natural colours or convert to grey tones. Enlarging the bark can create interesting graphic effects.

Cover a notebook by printing the design on to T-shirt transfer sheets. Iron on to pale fabric. Cut the fabric slightly larger than the book, spray glue on and fold over raw edges. Conceal them by gluing on the first and last page of the notebook.

### Deceptively dainty Crocus

The tender crocus is drawn towards the light. If it's too cold, it simply retreats. The stem of *Crocus tomasinianus* seems unfairly delicate, but this harbinger of spring is certainly no weakling.

### White blossom

A fluffy cloud of white blossom lightens up the garden. This Vibernum (right) blooms well into February and provides a beautiful prelude to spring.

### Out in the light

Frail Glory-of-the Snow (left) peep through an opening in the wall to receive their share of light. They are probably like the rest of us and badly need a dose of warmth and sunshine after a long, dark winter.

### Cyclamen in the snow

The smattering of snow that falls in Oxfordshire normally arrives in February just before the first signs of spring. Cyclamen (right) can withstand the snow and even manage to produce a fragile scent in the midst of the winter chill.

# Design & ideas

# Recipes